NEW
STEPS

PAUL GROVES · JOHN GRIFFIN

NATIONAL CURRICULUM · KEY STAGE 3

BOOK 1

LONGMAN GROUP UK LIMITED,
Longman House, Burnt Mill, Harlow,
Essex CM20 2JE, England
and Associated Companies throughout the world.

First published 1990

ISBN 0 582 05519 9

Printed and bound in Great Britain by
BPCC Hazell Books Ltd
Member of BPCC Ltd
Aylesbury, Bucks, England

THE NATIONAL WHAT?

A pupil's guide to the National Curriculum in English.

What is the National Curriculum?

If you looked up the words in a dictionary you would find:

national (a) public, general, applying to one's country.

curriculum (n) a course of study. So the National Curriculum is a course of study that is nation-wide – what every pupil in Britain should try to know and be able to do.

How does it work?

What sorts of skills would you most likely be learning in English?

English is about communication between people, whether you are reading your favourite author or explaining your illness to your doctor. A simple task such as this needs all the main English skills. To visit your doctor you might need to READ a bus timetable, the destination of the bus, the name of the road where the surgery is. Fortunately the chemist has to read the doctor's (usually) rotten HANDWRITING, but you will certainly need your skills of SPEAKING and LISTENING to explain what is wrong and listen to the doctor's advice. You'll need to fill in a form at the surgery (READING, UNDERSTANDING and WRITING) which won't impress the receptionist if it's untidy and full of crossings out (PRESENTATION) and inaccurate words (SPELLING).

So the National Curriculum for English will help you to improve in these areas: Reading, Writing, Speaking and Listening, Spelling, Handwriting and Presentation.

I've done all those already.

Yes, and that's one of several reasons why you shouldn't worry about the National Curriculum. But you can improve all of them, can't you?

Well, I'd do that without the National Curriculum, so what's new?

Have you made a radio play, written a story for young children, made a teenage magazine? Can you fill in a form as well as you can write a story, make an advert as well as you can write a business letter? Do you change what you say and how you say it according to your audience? Do you know what Standard English is? Are you interested in dialect and accent? Can you always find what you're looking for in your library? Do you always know what you are looking for? Do you know what present tense means, or narrative poem?

It's a poem that tells a story.

Ah, well you had me there. Good! But we've given you some idea of the range you'll cover. One of the big differences is that Speaking and Listening will count as much as Reading or Writing.

Count for what?

When you're assessed.

You mean tested. I thought you'd come to that.

It's not too bad, really. You'll follow the Programmes of Study, the kinds of things we've mentioned, and your teacher will keep some record of how you're progressing in the Attainment Targets – they're just checks that you've covered all the material. There are Attainment Targets for each of the five areas of English and you'll progress up them from Level 1 to Level 10.

That sounds very hard – I don't think I'll bother with it.

You have to; it's the Law. And it's not as complicated as it sounds. You've probably reached Level 3 for each of the targets already. You're starting a new stage (called a Key Stage) in your learning – it lasts until you're 14.

I have reason to believe you're not bothered with the National Curriculum.

I'm not happy about these Attainment Targets – they sound hard.

If you were sent to ask another teacher for 30 copies of 'Grinny' from the top shelf of the cupboard at the back of the room, would you return with the right books? If so, you would have satisfied one of the checks for Level 3 of the Speaking and Listening Attainment Target: 'Convey accurately a simple message.' You see, they're not as fierce as they sound.

You said I'm at a stage that lasts to 14. What then?

Key Stage 3, you're on. You have tests before going to Stage 4.

What! Tests! What Tests?

There are tests at 7, 11, 14 and 16. So you've missed two already. They're national tests; so everybody does them. And they will be just the kind of work you've been doing. You might make a poetry anthology, a magazine, some project like that – nothing very headbreaking, and probably enjoyable. They are checks on your ability in the Attainment Targets for Reading, Writing, Speaking and Listening.

You've forgotten Spelling.

No, I haven't. And even if I have, you've forgotten Handwriting. They're both important enough to have separate Attainment Targets, but of course there aren't as many Levels for you to progress through. Level 3 for Handwriting says: 'Begin to produce clear and legibly joined-up handwriting.' After that all you can do is concentrate on making your handwriting and presentation better.

I wrote on your essay 'Produce more fluent handwriting' as you well know

What do you mean, presentation?

The way you set out your work, the design of it. You might, for instance, be well into word-processing already. But that kind of skill is also important in the National Curriculum.

How about a quick re-cap?

Here goes, then:
You follow the Programmes of Study – lots of new and enjoyable work there. Your teacher keeps a check on your progress towards the Attainment Targets in:
  Speaking and Listening
  Reading
  Writing
  Handwriting
  Spelling

And I do separate pieces of work for all of these?

No, it can't work like that. Each assignment will be helping you to achieve in more than one area. For instance, if you'd looked up 'National Curriculum' yourself, you'd be using an 'appropriate information service' (a dictionary) helping you in the Reading target. If you could then explain 'National Curriculum' to your parents, you'd be practising one of the Speaking and Listening targets. If you knew that (a) after national in the dictionary meant 'adjective' and (n) after curriculum meant 'noun', you'd be showing knowledge of grammatical terms. So each piece of work will improve your ability in several ways.

So what are the other reasons I shouldn't worry?

Eh?

You said that I had many reasons not to worry. You've only said one.

You'll enjoy the work – that's another. You'll be doing more group work, drama, more talking (of the right sort!) – that's several more. And these checks and tests; all they're doing is giving you a chance to show off what you can do. They're not trying to catch you out, finding things you can't do. And, anyway, you'll be famous.

I don't believe you.

When you're 80, you'll say: 'Of course, I was the first to take the National Curriculum.'

Oh Yeah. And my grandchildren will say: The National What?

Oh, get on with the book.

Contents

1 **Different kinds of writing** 10
Try it youself 12

2 **A play to read and discuss** 13

The Giant Bat 13
Discuss the play in small groups 18
Look at the dramatic events 18

3 **What is a play?** 19

What makes a play interesting? 20
Discuss the plot 21
Making speech like real life – the apostrophe 21
Write your own play 21
Re-drafting 22
Record Sheet 23

4 **Looking at dialect** 25

The way we speak locally 25
Red Ridin' 'Ood 26
Red Riding Hood 27
Red Ridinud 28
Write a short fairy story 30
Word search 30
Hello, there! 30

5 **You and your library** 33

Reading materials 33
The parts of a book 34
Finding a fiction book 35

6 **How words work – nouns** 38

Words we can't do without 39
Make your own dictionary 41

7 What is poem? 42

Exactly like a 'V'   *Abram Bunn Ross*   42
Partners   *Judith Nicholls*   42
Late   *Judith Nicholls*   43
Old Hank   44
Prose or poetry?   44
Rhyme and rhythm   45

8 The language of poems 47

A narrative poem – for speaking aloud   47
The Day the Animals Talked   *Terry Jones*   48
Give a performance   52
Man in Zoo   52
What's it for?   53
Using everyday language   54
I Dreamt I Took Over My Secondary School   *Trevor Millum*   54
Sorting Him Out   55

9 Writing a story for young children 56

Mr Egbert Nosh   56
Finish the story   58
Think about layout and punctuation   58
Write your own children's story   59

10 How words work – proper nouns 61

What's in a name?   62

11 A personal story for your magazine 63

The Hags – A True Story   63
Role play   66
A sense of audience   66
Bias   66
Fact or fiction?   66

12 How to interview someone   67

Interview with a young person   67
Interview with an older person   68
Differences between the two interviews   69
Prepare your questions and make notes   69

13 Definitions – what words mean   71

Write your own definitions   71
The Definition Game   72
When a definition is not enough   72
The Adjective Game   73
The Invention of Adjectives   74

14 From spoken to written words – a transcription   76

Turn the transcript into a written story   77
Use a tape recorder   77
A little word of importance – pronouns   78

15 The language of forms and letters   79

Filling in forms   79
Make an address book   80
Write a friendly note   82
Setting out a letter   82
Write your own letters   84
A shopping survey   86

16 The language of selling   87

Looking at advertisements   87
Role play: using the telephone   88
Did you understand the message?   89
Advertising in the past   90
A radio advert   93

17 Characters in a story   94

William's Version   *Jan Mark*   94
Re-write a fairy tale   100

18   Get yourself heard   101

    Pollution problem   101
    Ideas about ID   102
    The Royals   102
    Bullying relief   102
    Why crimes should be punished more severely   103

19   How to use a thesaurus   104

    Pick the best word   104

20   Just as it happened   109

    Banjo   *Denis Foster*   109

DIFFERENT KINDS OF WRITING

1

In your National Curriculum course you will hear the word *language* used many times. Language is the words we speak and write down to help us to communicate with each other. As you know there are many different languages from many parts of the world, like French, Urdu and Chinese. There is also the sign language of the deaf.

In this book we will be concerned with helping you to use the English language – which is really a mixture of many languages – as well as you can, when you speak and when you write and read.

The more you look on language as a wonderful human invention, the better you will come to use it yourself. In other words, we want you to like words. In Step 1 we look at different kinds of writing.

⇨ How many different kinds of writing can you think of – the actual words, not the style of handwriting? There are certainly many different kinds of writing.
Look carefully at the fifteen examples here and on the next page. Then match the numbers with the letters to show you know the source of each piece of writing.

1   VICTORIA   I have never seen that knife before.
      DETECTIVE   Then how do you account for your initials being carved on the handle?
              (He shows Victoria the knife)

2 Add two ounces of flour and mix to a smooth paste.

3 'Take the second on the left and then turn right at the crossroads. It's next to the pub called "The Green Dragon".'

4 Once upon a time a woodcutter lived in a small cottage at the edge of the forest.

5 What's the difference between an elephant and a telephone box?

6 Good condition. £60 o.n.o.

7 People who are always praising the past
And especially the times of faith as the best
Ought to go and live in the Middle Ages
And be burnt at the stake as witches and sages.

8 'I did my homework, sir, but it got damaged. The cat did it. It wasn't my

fault. My dad should have let it out. I'll bring it when it's dry.'

9 IT'S AN OLD-UP!

Two pensioners tried to rob the Peterborough branch of the Halifax Building Society yesterday.

10 Your best friend comes from the hairdresser's looking hideous. Do you
   a) Pretend you haven't noticed?
   b) Say it's nice?
   c) Tell him he looks awful?
   d) Say 'Never mind; it will soon grow out.'?

11 Felly (n) one of the curved pieces in the circumference of a wheel.

12 'And ladies and gentlemen, who benefits from all this? Is it ordinary people, such as you and me? Is it the person in the street? Oh no, not on your life. You know who will take the profits, don't you? The same people who always take them. Yes, that's right.'

13 To be taken three times a day, after meals.

14 'Now I'm not asking £10, not even £5. Fifty pence a jar. I'm giving it away. How many would you like, sir? What about you, madam?'

15 Thank you very much for the socks. They were just what I wanted, especially the ones with green elephants on them. Auntie Kay sent me . . .

A A poem
B A recipe
C A thank-you letter
D A dictionary definition
E A newspaper article
F Instructions for taking medicine
G A play
H A fairy story
I An excuse
J Directions
K A political speech
L A market trader
M A quiz
O A joke
P An advert

In pairs, discuss your answers. You will probably have got most of these right. Discuss any you got wrong. Language can sometimes be confusing. Which ones are the most difficult to recognise? Decide how you knew any right answers. Is it simply what is said, or is it also how it is said? Look at the type of words used and the way they are set out. Decide with your partner how you can recognise each of these types of writing.

Deciding on the differences between a play and a story, between an advertisement and a recipe are quite easy. But there are also many differences within the same type of writing. How many types of story can you think of? Still in pairs, add to this list: Fairy, Detective, Adventure . . .

Try it yourself

▭▷ Choose three types of writing from the fifteen and write your own examples of each type. Write only a few lines for each. Swop with your neighbour. Can you recognise the types each of you has chosen?

FOOTNOTE

Different types of story, play and poem are called *genres* (pronounced jon-re). You will be asked to write in many different kinds of genre in this book.

You will have noticed that some of the different types of writing are examples of speech set down on a page. Still in pairs, go through the fifteen again and decide which are speech.

▭▷ Now make up a few words each that the following people might say. Put them in speech marks.

A A doctor
B A policeman
C A friend in the playground who has had his or her foot trodden on
D A headteacher
E A grandparent talking about the old days
F A young child
G The Queen

A PLAY TO READ AND DISCUSS

2

The aim of this book is to help you to develop your ability to speak and write in many different ways. Let us first look at a play.

Read this play to yourself. Then read it aloud in groups. A, B and C are children. Give them each a name before you start to read as a group. Note how the beginning of a play is set out, listing the cast and describing the scene. Notice the words in brackets which explain what the actors are to do or tell you the sounds that can be heard.

The Giant Bat

Cast:

A
B Three children
C

SCENE ONE – An old cottage. It is dark and creepy. The few bits of furniture are covered in dust.
(There is a sound of breaking wood. Then A, B and C enter slowly.)

A   Do you think we should?
B   Yeh, it's OK.
C   Keep us dry.
A   But it's breaking and entering.
B   Breaking? That bolt fell off in my hands.

C It doesn't look as if anybody has lived here for years.

A But it must belong to somebody. A farmer perhaps.

B Funny place to live, on the edge of a wood.

C Witches do.

A Don't, it's creepy enough as it is.

B Who believes in witches? Rubbish.

A There still are witches. I've read about it in the paper.

C Yes, a coven could meet here.
(Flash of lightning)

A Oh!

C The storm's started. Thank goodness we found this place in time. They say don't shelter under a tree in a storm. So we had to come in here as we were in the woods.

A Draw the curtains. I can't stand thunderstorms.

B Baby.

C I'll do it. Oh, they've come apart in my hands.

B The dust! (Goes into kitchen)

C Can't have been cleaned for years.

B (Off) The kitchen's as bad. No, I reckon someone's been living here. There are sacks on the floor and cider bottles.

c A tramp. I hope he's not upstairs. Listen.

A What?

c I thought I heard something.

A Did you?

B (Returning) The back door's locked.

A Did you hear a noise from upstairs?

B No.

c Must be the wind.

B Go and see.

c Not on my own.

B There would be footsteps in the dust on the stairs. No, no one's been up here.
   (Flash of lightning)

A Oh!

c No need to be scared, A. Lightning can't hurt us in here.

A Lightning can strike houses.

c It would strike the trees first.

B Just listen to that rain.

A It's raining cats and dogs.

c Funny expression that. You can't have cats and dogs in the air.

B You can have frogs.

c Frogs?

B I've read about it raining frogs.

c Rather spooky if it did.
   (Flash of lightning and thunder crash together)

A Oh, (Covering face in hands) that was right overhead.
   (The clock on the mantlepiece strikes seven. They stare at it)

c How come the clock's going, if nobody lives here?

B Could be a battery clock.

c No, look, there's a place to wind it.

B Someone must come here then.

A Don't.

B This place gets more spooky. I'll look upstairs.

A Dare you?

B I'm not scared of a tramp.

A But . . .

c This place gets more spooky. (B goes)

A I wish we could leave.

c We're not going out in that. Just listen.
   (Thunder. A light goes on in the room)

A Oh!

c It's got electricity then. B must have found the switch.

A I can't hear him. Do you think he's all right?

c B! B!

A He's not answering.
   (Moan comes from upstairs)

C B! Are you all right?

B (Leaping down the stairs) Ha. Ha! That put the wind up you, didn't it?

A It's bad enough as it is without you playing about.

A What's up there?

B Two rooms and an old bed.

C You found the electricity then?

B No.

C You must have switched something on.

B I didn't.

C But this light came on.

A He's fooling again.

B I'm not, honest.

C There must be somebody in the house with us.

B I've looked everywhere.

C Are you sure?

B Yeh.

A Let's get out of here. The lightning's stopped.

B Chicken!
(A faint whistling sound is heard)

C There is someone. Let's go. (They move to door)
This door. I can't open it. Someone's locked us in.

A Let me try. He's right.

B Leave it to me. Oh, the handle's come off in my hand.
(They come back in)

A (Going to window) Let's get out of here. (Screams)

C What is it?

A There's something big and furry on the window. I think it's a giant bat.
(Screams)

C Look it's flapping away.

B What a big one!

A We can't go out there.
(Whistling sound again)

C And we can't stay in here.

B This window's jammed. We'll try the one in the kitchen.
(They rush off)

A (Off) Oh, what can we do?

B Smash this window with a chair. That's what we can do.
(Sound of breaking glass)

B Come on.
(The light goes off as they go. The whistle comes again)

SCENE TWO – Outside in the wood.

C Look!

A Don't stop. That bat may come again.

C No, look.

B The house!

C It's going up in flames. The roof's all alight.

A We got out just in time.

C Those things must have been a warning to us.

B We could have been burnt alive.

A Let's run. We could be blamed for it. ˋ
(They run off)

SCENE THREE – A school classroom at break the next day.

A Look, this paper says the cottage in the woods burnt down. It says the farmer who owns it says he has seen strange lights there recently and heard strange sounds although no one has lived there for years.

C Look, it's called 'Witches Cottage'.

B And a man was murdered there in 1923.

A I knew there was something evil about it.

C A good job we got out in time.

A No more old cottages for me.

C Does it say anything about a giant bat?

A No, and we musn't either, or they'll blame us about the cottage.

Discuss the play in small groups

1 Look at the beginning of the play (up to the flash of lightning). How has the writer suggested that there is something spooky going on?
2 Look carefully at all of Scene One. When are the children frightened? Look at each scary happening. Which lines tell you that the children are afraid?
3 Would the play have been better if a witch or a ghost had appeared? Why or why not?
4 What if B had not come down from upstairs? How would this have changed the play? How could you have ended the play then?
5 How could Scene Two have been made more exciting?
6 What do you think of Scene Three, the ending of the play?
7 What do you think about the way the children talk? Does it sound like the way your friends talk? Would you alter any of the words?

6 The cottage burning down.

If the children found out that there was a normal explanation for the dramatic events, would it have spoiled the play?

Look at the dramatic events

There could be a normal explanation for each of the dramatic (exciting) events in the play:

1 The clock could have been started by the children walking about (clocks are temperamental).
2 The light switch was faulty and the storm caused a surge of power.

▭▷ How could you explain the other dramatic events?

3 The whistling.
4 The door not opening.
5 The bat.

WHAT IS A PLAY?

3

In this Step we think about plays as stories in which things people say are written down for the actors.

We also think about what makes a play exciting.

We then ask you to write your own play and give you a few tips about layout and punctuation.

Finally we start to encourage you to develop good spelling habits.

⇒ Working in pairs, choose one of the outlines below. One of you write the first ten lines of the outline as a play, the other write it as a story.

1 Three children are sitting in a park. Suddenly the earth beneath their feet starts to move. What is it? An earthquake? A creature from inner Earth? A prisoner escaping from a nearby gaol?

2 Three children on holiday at the sea go in a cave. A rock fall blocks the mouth of the cave. They explore to find another way out. But they soon hear a sound of music. What is it? What happens to them?

Compare what you have written. Together make a list of the differences between writing a play and a story. Here are some clues to help you. Each of the lines below is either part of a play or a story. It could not be both.

1 'Where are you going?' asked Whitney.
2 (She turns her back to him)
3 Caroline: I can't see the house from here.
4 They all lived happily ever after.
6 SCENE TWO: The Mistry's Front Room

FOOTNOTE

1 A play is a story performed by actors.
2 The storyline is called the *plot.*
3 The words the actors use are called the *dialogue.*
4 A written down play is called a *playscript.*
5 The words in brackets that tell the actors what to do (or explain what sounds can be heard) are called *stage directions.*
6 Plays are divided into *acts;* acts are divided into *scenes.* This is usually to show the action of the play has moved on in time or place.

What makes a play interesting?

A play can be set out correctly, be accurately written, but also be very boring. Why isn't this a good start to a play?

WOMAN It's a nice day today.

MAN Yes, it is.

WOMAN I thought it would be a nice day when I got up.

MAN So did I.

WOMAN The sun's hot already.

MAN Yes, it is.

WOMAN Won't want to do much today.

MAN No, you won't.

WOMAN It's better than yesterday.

MAN Yes, it is.

The problem with the beginning to this play is that it is not *dramatic.* Nothing happens.

This does not mean that each play needs to have a fight in it, but the *characters* or actors do need to argue, fall out, talk behind each other's backs so that we are interested enough to watch and listen. If some of the characters are unusual in any way so that we want to know more about them, this makes the play even more interesting. In all good plays there are characters we learn more about as the play progresses.

▭ Look back at the ten play lines you wrote at the beginning of this Step. Working in the same pairs, decide how these lines could be improved. Are any of the characters unusual? Is what the characters say interesting? Rewrite the ten lines so that they are more dramatic.

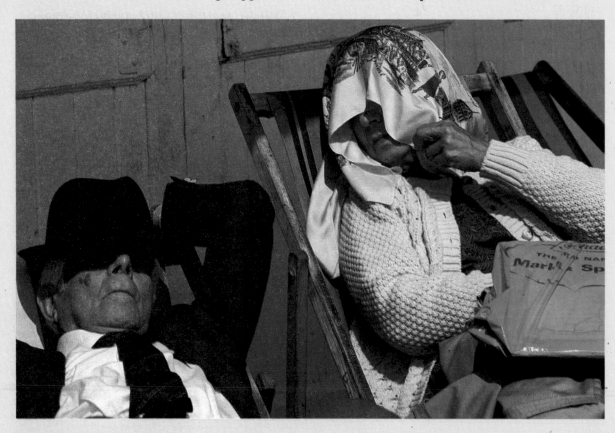

Discuss the plot

The plot of a play is what happens. It is the storyline. Lots of people like plays with strong plots. That means something interesting must happen to the characters like being in an aeroplane that has an engine on fire. Will the plane crash? Will some of the passengers panic?

▷ In pairs, tell each other the plot of the most exciting film or TV programme that you have ever seen. Explain what happens and why it is exciting.

▷ Write a paragraph outlining the plot of 'The Giant Bat' on page 13.

Making speech like real life – the apostrophe

Plays are speech. And speech needs to be like real life. Listen to people talk at school, and in shops and buses or at a party, for instance. Writers often copy down in a notebook things they hear people say.

Most people would not say:

'I *did not* win because I *had not* brought my proper running shoes.'

They would be more likely to say:

'I *didn't* win because I *hadn't* brought my proper running shoes.'

They would **abbreviate** (shorten) *did not* and *had not*. An **apostrophe** is used to show where a letter has been missed out. This is one use of the apostrophe – to show missing letters.

▷ Abbreviate these words. Make sure you place the apostrophe where the letter or letters have been missed out. For example, you punctuate *have not* as *haven't,* not *have'nt.*

could not	should not
did not	they have
do not	they are
has not	we will
have not	we are
I am	we have
is not	you will
it is	you are
I will	you have
must not	he will
may not	she will
might not	he is
shall not	she is

Write your own play

Now you are all ready to write a play of your own. There is a lot to remember so spend some time planning.

1 How many characters have you decided upon? More than three or four makes the play much more difficult to write.
2 Write the names and any interesting details about the characters before you start, for example:

    Zohra, aged 13 – always takes the lead, though she often leads the others into trouble.
3 Is the story of your play going to be a realistic one (perhaps about something that has happened to you or your friends) or will it be a ghost story, science fiction, or a mystery?
    There are lots of types (or genres) to choose from.
4 Who is your play for? Perhaps it could be for young children, people of your own age or something that might interest a particular group – a play about fishing or a sport, for instance. The people your play is aimed at are called your **audience.**

5 Where does the play take place? Will there be changes of place? Be sure to set out the acts and scenes clearly.
6 Will it take place in a few hours or will it stretch over several days?

⇨ Now write your play – good luck – You may be a future Shakespeare!

FOOTNOTE

Check the *layout* and *punctuation* of your play.

1 The layout is how your play is set out on the page. Have you told your audience where each scene is set? Have you started a new line with every change of speaker? Are stage directions in brackets? Look back to page 13 ('The Giant Bat') if you are unsure.
2 You do not need speech marks around the dialogue in your play, like you would need in a story. Cross them out if you have put them in.
3 There are often a lot of questions in speech. Check that you have put in all the question marks.
4 Make sure that people's names are spelt with capital letters for the first letter.
5 Do the sentences begin with a capital letter and end with a full-stop?
6 Have you checked the abbreviations you did on page 21?
7 Use a comma when someone is being directly addressed: Come here, O'Neill. James, are you there?

ASSESSMENT

After each longer piece of work, make a Record Sheet like the one shown opposite. This will help you to revise what you have learnt and to assess your progress over the course. It may help if you work in small groups of three or four. You could then read and comment on each other's work.

– – – – – – – – – – – – – – – –

Re-drafting

All writers make alterations to their first *drafts*, perhaps because they had second thoughts themselves, or perhaps in response to comments by other people. *Re-drafting* is not simply a matter of checking punctuation and spelling. You should always do this. Sometimes you might want to alter a whole section of your work. Here is an example.

In her Record Sheet, Julie mentions that the first part of her play was criticised. Imagine that this was what she wrote:

> SCENE ONE – Julie's bedroom. Julie and Michelle are looking out of the window.

MICHELLE	Well, we've skived lessons now. It was a long way to run, wasn't it.
JULIE	About half a mile, and we had to walk over the playground not to make them suspicious.
MICHELLE	I don't think anybody saw us.
JULIE	I hope my dad doesn't come back from work.
MICHELLE	Why should he come back? He doesn't usually come home early, does he.
JULIE	No, I don't think so.

Record Sheet

The task

Writing the play.

The preparation

We read a play called 'The Giant Bat' and discussed the play in small groups.
Wrote the beginnings of a play and a story in pairs.
Compared the two genres.
Learnt some technical words about plays and how to use apostrophes in our scripts.

Planning the task

I chose to call my play 'Bad Luck'. It would be about the time Michelle and I skived games and went to my house and my dad came home early from work and caught us. There are four characters: me, Michelle, my dad and my year tutor. There will be three scenes: (1) my house before we heard dad's car, (2) conversation with dad, (3) in Mrs Jacob's office. It will be a true play.

Writing the play

I found it hard to get started with the speech between Michelle and me. It was easier with my dad and Mrs Jacobs because I remembered a lot of what they said. I liked writing the play because it was all true.

Assessment

Three of us read each other's plays and talked about them. I was the only one to write a play from experience, though Jackie's play was about a ghost she had read about in a story. That was the most exciting play, but the other two thought mine was the most interesting.

Spelling and punctuation

We checked each other's spelling and punctuation. I'd missed out a lot of question marks.

Re-draft

I altered the first few lines where we wondered if my dad would come home early. It was better if it was just a shock when he did.

Imagine these were the criticisms of Julie's start:

1 The first two speeches are silly. They know they have skived and how far they have walked and run. So they wouldn't tell each other.
2 It's better if the dad turns up as a surprise. They shouldn't give the audience the idea that he might come home.

⇨ Re-draft the start of Julie's play to satisfy these two criticisms. Julie wants to tell the audience the girls are skiving lessons, but she needs to make the conversation sound more natural. What sorts of things might the girls say?

SPELL WELL

Some people can write brilliant stories, or talk very well but they have a poor visual memory which means they cannot see in their mind's eye the shape of a word or the order of the letters in it. Other people have difficulty because of hearing problems.

If you are a poor speller, do not despair. Many famous people have been poor spellers. But we now know that things can be done to help you. We have a plan to help you with your spelling problems.

In this book watch for the well signs. Inside each well will be a group of letters that often go together. This will help your visual memory. Your job is to add to the word family as many words as you can that are made from the letters. For example:

With this group you can make:
colour favourite journey our flour hour your neighbour flourish

Can you think of any others for this family?

▭ Keep your own dictionary, a page for each letter of the alphabet. Choose the two words you think you might find most difficult to spell from each family. In this case, for example, you might enter 'colour' under 'c' and 'favourite' under 'f'.

Here is one to start with:

With this group you can make:
mess necessary guess success essential stress

And here is one more:

With this group you can make:
each beach reach peach teach bleach

LOOKING AT DIALECT

4

In this Step we are going to look at your local speech by reading a story written in local dialects.

The way we speak locally

Because communications were bad earlier in our history – poor roads, no railways – and because of poverty, few people in Great Britain left the area they were born in. This meant that language developed differently in different areas of the country. These differences often depended on which invaders had come to the area to leave bits of their language behind them.

There were also no mass methods of communication like television and radio to spread methods of speaking. This led to the way we speak locally or dialect. Look at these three definitions:

Accent   Everybody has an accent. The sound of a voice is, if you listen carefully, just like a fingerprint. We all sound slightly different to one another. Not everybody, though, has a local accent, a tone or sound of voice that tells you they come from one particular area.

Dialect   Dialect is a use of words and sentence structure that often identifies you as having grown up in a particular part of the country.

Standard English   Standard English is a dialect. It was at one time the way of speaking in the South East part of the country. But now it is the form of language used for almost all types of communication in all parts of the country. So knowing Standard English is important.
You need to know Standard English, though there are times when a dialect might be preferable.
You need not adopt the accent usually linked with Standard English – as long as people can understand what you are saying.

Read the Welsh version of Red Riding Hood (page 26).

Red Ridin' 'Ood

Told by a mother to her little one, in the same manner as her mother in turn, used to tell it to her.

The little dwt was wanged out and getting crotchetty. "Come over by 'ere and cwtch up, and I'll tell you a story," said her mam. "'Eisht now, and I'll tell you all about Red Ridin' 'Ood in exactly the same way as *my* mam used to tell it to me...."

Once upon a time, there was a little bit of a girl called Red Ridin' 'Ood. She was only a little dwt, like you, and she lived with 'er mam and dad over by the forestry. 'Er dad worked days reg'lar in the forestry cuttin' trees down, and 'er mamgu lived a tidy step further on, on the other side of the forestry, like.

One day, 'er mammy asked Red Ridin' 'Ood to take some goods to 'er mamgu who 'ad been bard-in-bed and under the doctor frages. 'She'll be glad to 'ave these things in, 'cos she 'aven't been able to get about, poor dab. You'll go, won' you?'

'A course I will,' said Red Ridin' 'Ood.

'You better shape youerself then,' said 'er mam, 'cos it's a tidy step back and fore, and keep youer eyes open for that wicked wolf who do live over by there in the forestry!'

Red Ridin' 'Ood thought she better put on 'er red cloak and 'ood 'cos it might come on to rain nasty, and then, off she went, full fuss to 'er mamgu's....

Now, that wicked wolf 'ad gone over mamgu's, dragged 'er out of bed, shoved 'er out of the way, cwtched, so no one could see 'er, and 'e jumped into bed to take mamgu's place....

When Red Ridin' 'Ood got to mamgu's, she was out of puff with rushin' up the trip. She put the goods in the back kitchen and went into the middle room to see 'ow mamgu was gettin' on.

She sat down by the bed, looked at 'er mamgu, and thought, 'There's a funny jib on mamgu today....!'

She said, 'There's big eyes you got, mamgu'.

'That's so I cun see you tidy,' said the wolf.

'There's big ears you got,' said Red Ridin' 'Ood.

'Theyer, so as I cun 'ear you tidy,' said the wolf.

'There's big your mouth is!' said Red Ridin' 'Ood.

'That's by there for me to gobble you all up!' said the wicked wolf, an' 'e took 'olt of 'er cloak to ketch 'er! ...

Red Ridin' 'Ood was flabbergasted – it shook 'er rigid – but she was kokum. She shiggled 'er way out of that cloak an' was out of there like a winky. She went off, full pelt, along the road to where 'er father was 'ard at it. Talkin' twenty to the dozen she told 'im all that 'ad 'appened. 'E took 'is chopper, ran all the way back to mamgu's and gave that wolf a real belter!!

'E and Red Ridin' 'Ood got mamgu out of the cwtch under the stairs where the wolf 'ad put 'er. Mamgu was in 'er oils to be rescued, safe an' sound . . . . an' they all lived 'appy ever after . . . .

Now read the Standard English version of the same story.

Red Riding Hood

The little child was exhausted and miserable. "Come over here and snuggle up and I'll tell you a story," said her mother. "Be quiet now and I'll tell you all about Red Riding Hood in exactly the same way my mother used to tell it to me."

Once upon a time, there was a little girl called Red Riding Hood. She was only a little child, like you, and she lived with her mother and father by the forest. Her father worked every day in the forest cutting trees down, and her grandmother lived quite a long way away, on the other side of the forest.

One day her mother asked Red Riding Hood to take some provisions to her grandmother who had been ill and seeing the doctor for a long time. 'She'll be glad to have these things, because she hasn't been able to get about, poor thing. You'll go, won't you?'

'Of course I will,' said Red Riding Hood.

'You had better hurry up then,' said her mother, 'because it's a long way there and back, and keep your eyes open for that wicked wolf who lives in the forest.'

Red Riding Hood thought she had better put on her red cloak and hood because it might start raining hard, and then, off she went enthusiastically to her grandmother's . . . .

Now, that wicked wolf had gone to her grandmother's, dragged her out of bed, hid her so no one could see her, and he jumped into bed to take grandmother's place . . .

When Red Riding Hood got to her grandmother's she was tired out from rushing up the hill. She put the provisions in the kitchen and went into the middle room to see how her grandmother was getting on.

She sat down by the bed, looked at her grandmother, and thought, 'Grandmother looks strange today' . . .

She said, 'What big eyes you've got grandmother.'

'That's so I can see you well,' said the wolf.

'What big ears you've got,' said Red Riding Hood.

'They are so I can hear you well,' said the wolf.

'What a big mouth you've got,' said Red Riding Hood.

'That's for me to gobble you up!' said the wicked wolf, and the caught hold of her cloak.

Red Riding Hood was surprised – she was shocked – but she was crafty. She wriggled her way out of her cloak and was out of there very quickly. She ran along the road to where her father was busy working. Talking quickly she told him what had happened. He picked up his axe and ran all the way to grandmother's and struck the wolf . . .

He and Red Riding Hood helped grandmother out of the cupboard under the stairs where the wolf had put her. Grandmother was delighted to be rescued safe and sound and they lived happily ever after.

▷ Make two lists, one for the words in the Welsh version that you did not understand at all, and one for those you understood but do not normally use. For instance, from the first two lines your lists might be:

dwt	crotchetty
wanged	mam
cwtch	

Find the Standard English versions of the words you did not understand.

If you inserted the words you found into the Welsh tale, you still wouldn't have made a Standard English version. Look at these sentences, for instance:

That wicked wolf who do live over there by the forestry.
There's big eyes you got.

Put these sentences into Standard English and you will see that dialect is not simply using different individual words. It is an individual, distinct manner of speech – a different language with its own word order and grammar.

Now look at a Leicestershire version of the same story.

Red Ridinud

Once upon a time . . . it were a satdy . . . Little Red Ridinud were off to tek some sarnis to 'er Gran's cos she were badly. Nipping through Abbey Paark, she were picking a few flaaz; keeper were a mate of 'er Dad's, so she didn't reckon it'd marrer.

"Ay oop, mi duck. Where yer gooin'?"

Looking up she saw a gret wolf stannin' there gawpin'atta.

"Um gooin' Gran's," she said, "and it int no business o yourn neither."

"Canna come wiya?" he asked. "I into doin nowt satdy."

Red Ridinud weren't 'avin none o that. Her mam'd towd 'er never twav nowt to do wi' strangers.

"No," she snapped. "I int gooin' wi' nubdy."

"Worrayer gorrin that plaggy bag?" wolf kep on. "Giss summat teat. Um starved."

"Oo-yer," she exclaimed. "You an arf gorralorragob! I int gorroat, so shift out mi way. I gorra meckayste."

"Wotsamarrer weeyar, yer mardy cat?" wolf yawped as he sloped off.

'E knew where Gransous were so 'e legged it like 'ell and got there fust, tied owd gel up and shoved 'er in cupboard. Owt furra laff, he thorght and 'opped into bed.

When Red Ridinud arrived and clapped eyes on wolf in Gran's bed, she were frit. "Oo, 'Gran," she said. "Wot's up? You en arf got big ears."

"All the berrar twear yer wi', mi duck," wolf said.

Red Ridinud felt gooey numb. "Gran, you en arf got big eyes."

"All the berrer to see yer wi', mi duck," come the reply.

"But Gran," Red Ridinud stammered, "Ayyer bin dentist? You en arf got big choppers."

Leappin' outer bed, wolf cried: "All the berrer tweat yer wi', mi duck," and copped holt o Red Ridinud.

"'Ello, 'ello, 'ello. What's gooin' on 'ere then?" a deep voice called, and in walks park keeper.

Ooyer. It were a near goo wi' that wolf. Lessope beak gizzim six month!

▭ In small groups, discuss 'Red Ridinud'.

1 Which phrases represent accent only, for example, 'a few flaaz'?
2 Which are dialect words, for example, 'Yer mardy cat'? Can you guess what 'mardy' means?
3 Which are dialect forms, for example, 'It *were* a satdy'? What is the Standard English word needed instead of 'were'?
4 Compare the Welsh and Leicestershire versions. What are their different ways of using language? For example, 'it shook 'er rigid' and 'gooey numb' are the dialect expressions for 'surprised'.

Write a short fairy story

▭ Try to make a local accent and dialect form of a fairy story. For example:

So this ere owd witch goes to the mirrer: 'Who do you reckon is the good-lookingest?' And the mirrer it goes: 'Well, you were but . . .

Record your version for the rest of the class to hear.

Word search

You recognised some of the local dialect words because they spread to other parts of the country. But many English words come from further away – from France and Italy, from the Romans and the Greeks.

For instance, many of our words connected with music were imported from abroad. If you looked up the word *music* in a large dictionary, you would find at the end of the definitions:

L musica   Gr mousiké.

This means the word 'music' comes from Latin, and the Romans took it from the Greeks. (The Romans conquered the Greeks and when they invaded Britain they brought

their own, and Greek words they adopted, into our language.)

▭ Find out how these words came into our language:

choir concert recorder hymn
trumpet stereo piano flute opera
instrument

Hello, there!

In this book you will continually be asked to look for the 'right' words – the ones that suit the occasion and the person you're speaking to. In many ways you do this already, for instance in how you greet the variety of people you meet every day.

In the Leicestershire version of the story, the wolf greets Red Riding Hood like this: 'Ay oop, mi duck.' In the Welsh version, Red Riding Hood calls her grandmother 'mamgu' and her mother 'mam'. What do you say when you meet people you know? What do they say to you? Here are some examples:

'Wotcha, Gramps.' – 'Hello, love.'
'Hi there, Nan.'   – 'Hello, blossom.'
'Morning, Sir.'   – 'Morning, George.'

▭ Use the diagram opposite to write in the greetings you give and receive from different people. You are in the middle. The six faces could be your relatives, friends, teachers. Choose the six for which you have a definite form of greeting. Put the greetings in the arrows. Name each of the faces. Then compare your greetings with other people's. What does each greeting show about the relationship?

Do not mark in this book in any way.

ASSESSMENT

Make a Record Sheet for this task, like the one you prepared when writing your play (see page 23). Record what you have learnt about accent, dialect and Standard English. Comment on your attempt at local dialect. Was your fairy story understood? Was it funny? Did your classmates think you used dialect well?

FOOTNOTE

You may need to discuss with your teacher how to write down your own local dialect, if it is a strong one.

1 Dialects that leave off the letter 'h' are written like this:

   'er – for *her*   *'ello* – for *hello*

   Use the apostrophe whenever you leave out a letter.

2 Words can be spelt as they sound:

   satdy – for *Saturday*
   Lessope – for *Let's hope*

3 Remember that dialect is not just a matter of different words. The word order may change and dialect forms may be used:

   "What's goin' on 'ere then?" a deep voice called and *in walks park keeper*.

▷ When should you use Standard English? For example, how does a newscaster speak? Think about writing and speaking. Discuss this in class.

▷ Get a blank map of Great Britain and put in the dialects (very roughly according to region). Here are some for you: Geordie, Glaswegian, Yorkshire, Cockney, Lancashire, Liverpudlian, Cornish, Somerset, Welsh . . . Make a list of the dialects you like to hear.

YOU AND YOUR LIBRARY

5

In this Step you will be introduced to the types of reading materials found in libraries. We will look at the parts that make up a book and do an exercise on alphabetical order.

Reading materials

There are four types of reading materials in most libraries. Look at the four groups below and see if you can add two titles for each group.

Fiction
Fiction books are stories that have been made up, for example:
> *Double Love* by Francine Pascal
> *Charlie and the Chocolate Factory* by Roald Dahl
> *The Weathermonger* by Peter Dickinson
> *The Pinballs* by Betsy Byars

▭ Now add two fiction books of your own.

Non-fiction
Non-fiction books are true books, topic books, project books, fact books or information books, for example:
> *Sikh Festivals* by Dr Sukhbir Singh Kapo
> *Smoking – What's in it for you* by Sue Armstrong
> *The Repair of Vehicle Bodies* by A Robinson
> *The Story of Pop* by John Byrne

▭ Add two non-fiction books of your own.

Reference
Reference books are non-fiction books which cannot be borrowed, but which are simply referred to for information, for example:
> *Encyclopaedia Britannica*
> *The Oxford English Dictionary*
> *Roget's Thesaurus*
> *The Guinness Book of Records*

▭ Add two reference books you can find in your library.

Periodicals
This means newspapers and magazines, for example:
> The *Daily Mirror*
> The *TV Times*
> *Practical Computing*
> *Early Times*

▭ Add two periodicals of your own.

The parts of a book

Everyone knows what a book looks like. But do you know the names of all the parts of a book? Here they are.

Author
The author of the book is the person who wrote it.

Title
The title is the name of the book.

Publisher
The publisher is the firm that publishes the book.

Book jacket
The jacket or cover of a book will include details of the author, title and publisher.

Spine
The spine is the backbone of the book that holds it together.

Spine labels
Spine labels are normally found on non-fiction library books and show the classification number used by the library.

Title page
On the title page, normally the first one inside a book, details can be found of the author, title, illustrator, editor, series and publisher.
On the back of this or on the same page you can find out the date a book was published which shows you if a book is out-of-date. You also find the ISBN. This is the number by which each book is identified in a publisher's catalogue.

Contents list
The contents list is normally found at the front of the book and it provides a guide to the information in the book by listing chapter titles and the pages they start on.

Index
The index is found at the back of a book and it is an alphabetical list of subjects covered in the book with page numbers.

▭ Choose a non-fiction book to work with. Then see how many of these questions you can do. Refer back in this book if you need to.

1 Write down the title of your book.
2 Write down the author of your book.
3 Write down the publisher of your book.
4 When was the book first printed?
5 What is its ISBN?
6 Look at the list of contents. How many chapters are there?
7 What is Chapter 3 called? Where does it begin?
8 Does the book have an index? If so, on what page?

▭ Look at these funny book titles.

Cliff Tragedy by Eileen Dover
Santa Claus by Mary Christmas
Gambling by Mustapha Bet
Acne by Ivor Spot
Do it yourself by Andy Mann
Dogs by Norah Bone

Can you make one up?

Finding a fiction book

The fiction books are arranged
alphabetically according to the author's
surname. It's important to know exactly
how *alphabetical order* works for this and
for many other reasons, for example using a
dictionary. Here are some quick tasks to
help you check your skill at using the
alphabet and putting things into
alphabetical order.

CODE

A	B	C	D	E	F	G	H	I	J	K	L	M	N
1	2	3	4	5	6	7	8	9	10	11	12	13	14

0	P	Q	R	S	T	U	V	W	X	Y	Z
15	16	17	18	19	20	21	22	23	24	25	26

MESSAGE

8 1 22 5   25 15 21   18 5 1 4   20 8 5   20 21 18 2 21 12 5
14 20   20 5 18 13   15 6   20 25 11 5   20 9 12 5 18   2 25
7 5 14 5   11 5 13 16 ?   9 20' 19 1   18 5 1 12 12 25
7 15 15 4   2 15 15 11.

▷ Use the code to decode the above
message.

▷ Now write a secret message of your
own using the same code. Try it out on a
friend.

▷ Put the following words into
alphabetical order:

frightful
league
anchor
promise
upbringing
basket
temptation
dolphin
whitewash
menu

▷ If words begin with the same letter
they have to be put in order using the
second letter as well. If the second letter is
the same, the third is used, and so on. Now
put the words below into alphabetical
order.

science
sandwich
scold
Saturday
scissors
saddle
sheep
scone
scandal
scarf

⟹ List these authors in alphabetical
order of surname which is the way authors
are listed in any library.

Nicholas Fisk
Michael Rosen
Betsy Byars
Paul Zindel
Katherine Paterson
Roald Dahl
Robert Leeson
John Branfield
Russell Hoban
Raymond Briggs

⟹ Imagine you have just written a fiction
book. Design a book jacket for it, using
Joanne's as a guide (opposite).

Front Flap

The author has drawn together the elements of fact and fiction in a unique combination both children and adults will appreciate
The Observer

An excellent book!
The Sun

Compares favourably with fiction giants such as 'Watership Down' and others.
Literary Press

£9.75

Front Cover

⊕FOXTROT⊕

ONE OF THE
'LIFE IN THE DAY OF...'
SERIES

AS SEEN ON T.V.

Spine

FOXTROT – 'LIFE IN THE DAY OF...' SERIES [4]

Jo Silvester

Back Cover

'Step! Don't go another step further! Wait 'til I get there! There are cruel, dangerous creatures with loud voices and rolling, fast legs that roam along that path!' Alice cried. 'Please not another victim of the Beasts' she thought.

One of her children had already been brutally snatched away from her and another killed by huntsmen, but she couldn't bear to think about that now.

Not when more lives were at risk!

© J. Silvester 1984

Back Flap

PHOTO

Although brought up in Cambridgeshire Jo now lives and works in Kent. This is the fourth book in her famous 'Life in the Day of' series. Previous titles are 'Bunny Hop', 'Stag Hunt' and 'Pound Puppy' and are published in 'Children's Press'. Jo has two or three more books in the pipeline.

HOW WORDS WORK ~ Nouns

The more you get interested in words and how words work, the better you will be at English.

In this book there are Steps about the way words work. They will help you to understand they all have particular jobs to do in sentences. The first kind of words we look at are called nouns.

In pairs, write a message (without letting your partner see) and try to make her or him understand your message by using only a quarter of the words. For example:

Message
'I have to take my sister to the dentist tomorrow so I will not be able to hand in my homework until Friday.'

You would be allowed five words (Which ones would you choose?) to get your message across. The rest you would do by gestures – pointing or nodding and shaking your head. Your partner can speak as much as she or he wishes. You have succeeded when your partner can say your message.

▭ Make a list of words the class used in their messages. What have they in common? Are most of them naming words, for example, sister, dentist, homework, Friday?

Naming words are called *nouns.*

Words we can't do without

Here are words from an English/Polish dictionary for English speaking holiday-makers:

English Word	Polish Word	Prounciation
address	adres	ad-res
aeroplane	somolot	sa-mo-lot
airport	lotnisko	lot-nees-ko
banana	banan	ba-nan
bank	bank	bank
beach	plaza	pla-zha
bread	chleb	hleb
car	wóz	vooz
cat	kot	kot
cinema	kino	kee-no
coach	autokar	a-oo-to-kar
dirty	brudny	brood-ni
dog	pies	pyes
doctor	doktor	dok-tor
England	Anglia	an-glya
envelope	koperta	ko-per-ta
February	Luty	loo-ti
fish	ryba	ri-ba
fly	mucha	moo-ha
God	Bog	boog
good	dobry	do-bri
holiday	urlop	oor-lop
hotel	hotel	ho-tel
handbag	torebka	to-rep-ka
ill	chory	ho-ri
insect	insekt	een-sekt
jumper	sweter	sve-ter
jacket	marynarka	ma-ri-nar-ka
July	Lipiec	lee-pyets
key	klucz	klooch

knife	noz	noozh
large	duzy	doo-zhi
lavatory paper	papier toaleta	pa-pyer to-a-le-ta
leg	noga	no-ga
lunch	obiad	o-byad
minute	minuta	mee-noo-ta
near	bliski	blees-kee
new	nowy	no-vi
old	stary	sta-ri
pain	ból	bool
passport	paszport	pash-port
Poland	Polska	pol-ska
pound	funt	fovnt
radio	radio	ra-dyo
room	pokoj	po-kooy
road	droga	dro-ga
Saturday	sobota	so-bo-ta
sharp	ostry	os-tri
shoe	but	boot
shop	sklep	sklep
stamp	zmaczeh	zna-chek
telephone	telefon	te-le-fon
tomorrow	jutro	yoot-ro
trousers	spodmie	spod-nye
voice	glos	gwos
village	wies	vyesh
waiter	kelner	kel-ner
weather	pogod	po-go-da
wrong	zly	zwi
zoo	zoo	zo-o

▭▷ Do the following exercise in pairs.

1 Write a message for your partner to de-code using at least six Polish words. For example:

A brudny pies came into my pokoj, ate the ryba I was having for obiad and bit my noga.

What does this mean? All the Polish words used are nouns except one. Which isn't a naming word?

2 With the pronunciation column on the right, try to give a simple message to your partner in Polish, using three nouns.

Nouns are the words we cannot manage without. Language must have started with people naming things:

Eight out of ten of the words in the Polish dictionary that our sample was taken from are nouns. They would be the most useful words for travellers.

⇨ Look in an English dictionary and notice that the letter *n* is put after a word that is a noun. How quickly can you find ten nouns beginning with the letter 'a'?

Make your own dictionary

⇨ Make a list of the words you would need for something that interests you like a hobby. (Do not write the definitions – what the words mean – yet.) Your dictionary could be: A Fishing Dictionary, A Dictionary of School Terms, A Shopper's Dictionary.

Write the twenty words that you think would be most useful and put them in alphabetical order. Notice how this is done by looking at the order of the English words in the Polish dictionary list. Six words are not in the right place. Can you spot them? You will need to look carefully and, in each case, you will need to go further than the first letter, for example, 'apple' would come before 'apricot' in a dictionary of fruits.

⇨ Try to give your partner a message using only words from your dictionary. How many of the words in your dictionary were nouns?

Most of our words today were brought by the invading tribes of Angles and Saxons in the fifth and sixth centuries AD. These are some of the earliest nouns to settle in England: day, night, light, dawn, sheep, swine, sun, moon, ox.

WHAT IS A POEM ?

7

In this Step we take a look at some poems.

You can recognise a poem as easily as you can spot a dog. They come in all shapes and sizes, but they can't disguise themselves.

Look at the pieces here and on page 44. How can you spot the one that isn't a *poem*?

Partners

Find a partner,
says sir, and sit
with him or her.
A whisper here,
a shuffle there,
a rush of feet.
One pair,
another pair,
till twenty-four
sit safely on the floor
and all are gone
but one –
who stands,
like stone,
and waits;
tall,
still,
alone.

Judith Nicholls

Exactly like a 'V'

When my brother Tommy
Sleeps in bed with me
He doubles up
And makes
himself
exactly
like
a
V

And 'cause the bed is not so wide
A part of him is on my side.

Abram Bunn Ross

Late

You're late, said miss.
The bell has gone,
dinner numbers done
and work begun.

What have you got to say for yourself?

Well, it's like this, miss.
Me mum was sick,
me dad fell down the stairs,
the wheel fell off me bike
and then we lost our Billy's snake
behind the kitchen chairs. Earache
struck down me grampy, me gran
took quite a funny turn.
Then on the way I met this man
whose dog attacked me shin –
look miss, you can see the blood,
it doesn't look too good,
does it?

Yes, yes, sit down –
and next time say you're sorry
for disturbing all the class.
Now get on with your story,
fast!

Please miss, I've got nothing to write about.

Judith Nicholls

The June grass, amongst which I stood, was taller than I was, and I wept. I had never been so close to grass before. It towered above me and all round me, each blade tattoed with tiger-skins of sunlight.

(Laurie Lee)

Old Hank

For a lark,
For a prank,
Old Hank
Walked a plank.
These bubbles mark
    O
    O
    O
    O
    O

Where Hank sank.

Anonymous

Prose or poetry?

The one you picked written in sentences and in a paragraph is said to be written in **prose**. Prose is the normal language of stories, newspaper articles, letters and reports.

▷ Try to make the prose piece into a poem. You can do this by shape or the length of the lines. Of course, the shorter the line the more you notice the words in it. Which words do you want to stress in this way?

▷ Compare your piece with your neighbour's or the rest of your group. Have you split up the sentences in similar ways? Are your pieces better than the prose? Which of the poems do you like best? Why?

Two of the poems on pages 42 and 44 have a special shape. Which ones are they? Does the shape have anything to do with what the poem is about?

▷ Write your own poem with a shape. You will probably find it easier to do if you stick to a subject you know best, like school or home.

Rhyme and rhythm

Rhymes are words that sound the same. Look at the poems on pages 42 and 44. Notice how *wide* rhymes with *side,* and *Hank* rhymes with *prank, plank* and *sank.* Look at the following examples.

The trouble with a kitten is
That
Eventually it becomes a
CAT

Ogden Nash

The trouble with kittens is that in the end they become cats.

▭ Why is the prose version not as interesting? How has Ogden Nash stressed the important word in three ways?

Teacher, teacher don't be dumb
Give me back my bubble gum.

Count the *syllables* in each line. A syllable is the smallest unit of speech. (Asleep is two sounds: *a-sleep.* Ground is one sound. Horrible is three sounds: *ho-ri-bull.*) If you do not understand work some out with your teacher. There are many poems made worse because the poet could not count the syllables he or she had used.

▭ Has the poet made a clear *rhythm* in the bubble gum poem? What do the number of syllables tell you? What if you had more in the first line than the second?

Kiss me now
Kiss me cunning
Kiss me quick
Mother's coming.

▭ How is the last line a contrast to the first three?

This is the night mail crossing the border
Bringing the cheque and the postal order.

W.H. Auden

What does the rhythm make you think of?

Young Johnson, whose first name was Paul
Just narrowly missed a bad fall.
He broke several teeth
And the jawbone beneath
Seven ribs, and a leg, but that's all.

This funny poem is called a *limerick.* Count the syllables in each line. Then look at which lines rhyme and make some rules for limerick writing.
Which word comes as a shock in the poem? How has the poet made it stand out?

▭ Write a prose version. Why isn't it as good?

⇨ Write your own limerick, paying attention to the rules you made up for limericks.

⇨ Put in the missing rhyme words in this poem by Robert Louis Stevenson.

We built a ship upon the stairs
All made of the back-bedroom ___
And filled it full of sofa ___
To go a-sailing on the billows.

We took a saw and several ___
And water in the garden pails
And Tom said, 'Let us also take
An apple and a slice of ___
Which was enough for Tom and ___
To go a sailing on, till tea.

NB: A sofa is a settee.

A pail is a bucket.

SPELL WELL

sound wound round mound bound
found foundation

region legion suspicion conception

trail bail rail railway hail tail tailor

Which of these words rhyme?

THE LANGUAGE OF POEMS

8

Back to that word *language* again. Do you need special language for poetry? Did you know that you can use words and phrases that you hear every day and shape them into poems? In this Step you will be asked to read a long poem about animals which we think you will enjoy. Do we take animals for granted? We ask your views on this.

Then we will look at the language of poetry by reading two poems that use words and phrases we hear all the time.

A narrative poem – for speaking aloud

Poems usually describe a feeling or a thought, but they can also tell a story – a *narrative.*

Read the following narrative poem by Terry Jones. Look at the rhythm and the rhymes in the poem. Notice the way the animals speak in everyday English.

Then choose people for the different parts. You will need:

a narrator (who does most of the speaking), a goldfish, dog, cat, budgie, mouse, goose, bison, deer, lion, leopard, minx, bear, musk deer, fox, crocodile, elephant.

The Day the Animals Talked

I woke up one morning
When the sun was high,
And I thought: 'Something's up!'
Though I didn't know why.

I got out of bed,
Then I went white as chalk,
For I suddenly heard
My goldfish talk.

Ah You've got up at last
And about time it said.
I've been swimming all night,
While you've been in bed

Well! You can imagine
My utter surprise;
I didn't believe
My ears or my eyes.

I was going to exclaim:
'Did *I* hear *you* talk?'
But just then the dog said:
'I need a walk!'

I turned and saw Rover
(Imagine the shock)
As he said: 'A good long one –
Not once round the block!'

I thought: 'This is crazy!'
But more was to come . . .
When I started to answer,
I found I was dumb!

I spluttered and pointed
And tried to say Wait
But nothing came out,
And the cat muttered Great

'The Boss has gone mute on us!
Just what we need!
How's he going to buy catfood?'
'And what about seed?'

This was the budgie,
Pacing its cage,
And who all of a sudden
Flew into a rage:

Lemme out You sadist
It pecked at its bell.
I can't bear this prison
My life here is hell

I tried to say 'Sorry!'
But nothing came out,
Then it was the goldfish
Who'd started to shout:

What about me
I'm stuck in this bowl
With nowhere to hide
Not so much as a hole

'Don't you think *I* go crazy?
I'm stared at all day
By that monster!' But Ginger
The cat looked away.

And I tried to say: 'Pets!
Please listen to me!'
But I was as dumb
As *they'd* been previously.

'You listen to us,
For a change!' said a mouse
Who appeared on a cupboard
'We live in this house,

'Yet you fill it with traps,
And you poison my young!'
And the others all murmured:
'He ought to be hung!'

But Rover stood by me,
And said: 'Listen here!
It may be the Master
Has just no idea

'Of half of the things
That go on in his name . . .'
The cat said: 'Let's show him!'
The rest said: 'We're game!'

So the animals dragged me
By beak and by paw
To the zoo, and I couldn't
Believe what I saw:

All the cages were open
The creatures roamed free,
And walked on their hind legs
Like you and like me.

When they saw me, they started
To scream: 'One's got loose!'
'That's a dangerous animal!'
Clamoured a goose.

'They've cooked all my ancestors,
Thousands a year!'
'And mine!' cried a bison.
'And mine!' sighed a deer.

And the animals started
To bellow and roar,
Till the lion held up
An immaculate paw:

'Now listen! A lot of us
Hunt for our meat.
This creature's no different.
His kind have to eat.'

'But they torture us, lion!'
The goose again crowed.
'They force us to feed
Till our livers explode!'

'Is this *possible*, Man?'
The lion turned to me,
And I couldn't deny it
(Nor could I agree).

And the murmur of horror
Turned into a roar,
As the leopard sprang up
And growled: 'I hate him more!

'At least the Man eats
The geese that he kills –
My kind he pursues
For his fashions and frills!'

'That's right!' cried the mink
And the seals and the bears.
'Who wants to be murdered
For something *he* wears?'

'And us, dears!' the musk deer
Were whispering as well.
'We're slaughtered merely
Cause men like our smell!'

'Ah! My friends! This is nothing!'
The fox had begun,
'Men hunt us poor foxes
Simply for *fun*!'

The babble of voices
Arose to the skies,
And the lion turned to me
With tears in his eyes.

'Oh, Man!' he said sadly,
'What have you to say?'
And I stood there as dumb
As a bottle of hay.

'Make him into a hand-bag!'
The crocodiles croaked.
'Turn him into a hat-stand,'
The elephants joked.

And the lion said: 'Oh, Man!
How *could* you have done
All these terrible things
By the light of the sun?

'You're found to be guilty!
You have no excuse,
And your punishment shall
Be pronounced by the goose!'

Then the animals bickered
And cried: 'No! Let me!'
But the goose cackled: 'Listen!
Here's what it shall be!

'Let's leave him to stew
On his own for a bit,
Then we'll pluck him and gut him
To roast on the spit!'

But the rest started screeching
With different ideas,
And I dropped to my knees,
With my hands on my ears.

Then I felt myself lifted
And thrown in a cage,
And I lay there in terror
For what seemed an age . . .

I awoke all alone.
Above me – the stars –
When I suddenly heard
A quiet tap on the bars,

And there was old Rover
At my cage's doors,
Concern in his eyes
And a key in his jaws.

'Come on, Master,' he grumbled,
While everyone sleeps,
'Let's get out of here
– this place gives me the creeps!'

He opened the cage
And I licked his dear face,
And I kept close to heel,
For I felt in disgrace.

And when we got home,
He put me to bed
Under the table,
And gently he said:

'Goodnight, old fellow.'
In his kindly tone,
And he patted my head,
And he gave me a bone.

And I settled right down,
And I slept like a log,
Thinking: 'Golly! I'm happy
I'm only a dog!'

Give a performance

⟹ Try a second reading, making it more
dramatic by having the main reader in the
centre of the room with all the animals
around her or him, taking a menacing step
forward while they say their lines. There are
opportunities for all the animals to speak or
make noises at once, for example:

And the murmur of horror
Rose into a roar

But the rest started screeching
With different ideas

Man in Zoo

▭ Animals in zoos have their cages labelled, describing their habitats (where they live), what they eat, their characteristics. Make a cage label for a man or a woman. Are they dangerous? Should the public be allowed to feed them?

▭ Use one of these pictures to write your own zoo poem.

FOOTNOTE

Did you notice that when each animal spoke the actual words used were enclosed in *speech marks?* They have been deliberately left out of verses 3, 8, 11 and 13.

Write these out putting in the speech marks and any punctuation marks you think are needed. There are several exclamation marks (because the animals are angry) and one question mark to be put in. Do this and then discuss with a group these things:

Why are speech marks helpful to a reader?
When do you use exclamation marks?
When do you use question marks?

What's it for?

Do you think the poem is meant to be funny or has it a serious point?

▷ On your own, reply to this children's newspaper article by someone of your own age, agreeing or disagreeing and giving, like Susan, examples to support your ideas.

Susan Rhodes, 12, from Essex

CONTRARY TO SUSAN RHODES' LETTER, YOU REALLY SPOIL THAT ANIMAL...

I AM writing this article to show my anger about how we take animals for granted.

I'm sure that none of the readers would like to be bullied by a bunch of big kids. So, why should we do it to animals?

Would you like to go home every night to a warm loving house? Or would you like to live the way some animals live? By this I mean being stuck in a cage and cramped all day, having tags put around your neck and needles stuck into you by huge people all day long.

Also would you like to have perfumes, lipsticks and eyeshadows wiped all over you to see if it has any bad effects on you.

I am also showing my anger over how we treat them for pleasure. Bull fighting for instance – when an animal is put in a ring to be tortured and killed.

I also heard about a TV programme that said that in certain countries dogs had bombs put around their necks which were blown up in enemy territory.

What have animals done to deserve this?

Using everyday language

Now read two poems that use words and
phrases we hear all the time.

I Dreamt I Took Over My Secondary School

I dreamt I took over my secondary school:
Sacked the Headmaster for breaking the rules,
Kept the Teachers outside during break in the cold
And took all their cigarettes: *You're really too old*
To be smoking – haven't you learnt yet, I said.
Learn to say no; you're too easily led!
I told them to stop talking and messing about,
The staff room's a cess pit. Get it cleaned out!
And, Deputy, don't drive that car like a bat out of hell –
Wait in the car park till the end-of-school bell.
I called in the matron and checked them for nits,
Tested their eyes and then tested their wits.
Gave the staff an IQ test, kept them in after school;
Made them read out their answers so they'd each feel a fool.
I sent several home to change shirts or their ties
Or put on dull dresses of more suitable size.
I gave lots of homework, which I didn't explain –
They put up their hands and asked questions in vain.
You should have been listening, I said with a smile;
Hand in tomorrow. Now line up in single file!
I ignored their excuses that they had to go out,
Your work must come first! I said with a shout.
Reports will be issued at the end of the term –
If you've not shown improvement, I'll have to be firm:
It may be the thumbscrews, it may be the rack ...
I'm going to wake up now ... but I'll be back!

Trevor Millum

Sorting Him Out

He's late again, you'll have to sort him out.
I'll try, but he's at such a tricky age.
If only he would buckle down to work.
If only he would tell us what he's doing.
I'm sure we've always done our best for him.
I'm sure he thinks that money grows on trees.
I bet he's had to stay behind again.
I bet he's eaten chips and sweets for dinner.
He says he wants a music centre now.
He says he wants a party for his mates.
He's coming now – *I'll leave it up to you.*
I'll do my best, but chip in when you can.

Don't you 'hello' me
In that tone of
Voice!
What time do you call
This?
I'll give you
Music centre!
Don't you be smart with
Me!
Do you think we're
Stupid?
If you think you're having your friends
Carrying on and messing up this house
You've got
Another think
Coming!
That's right, that's right
Go off and
Sulk!

I hope I've not got him upset again.
He needs to show us both the right respect.
There's just one thing I'd really like to ask.
I'll tell you anything you want to know.

Mum, was he like this when you
Married him?

Read the poem out loud in pairs. Then pick out the words and phrases from these poems that are often said by teachers and parents to children. How many of them have been said to you?

There must be some special ones that you hear every day that are not in either poem. Write them down. Then make your personal version of one of the poems. You can make yours more straightforward, if you wish. It need not be a dream or have a surprise ending. Notice how one poem uses rhyme and the other repetition. Here is one way you might start.

Now, if I told you
ONCE
I've told you a
HUNDRED TIMES
Do not . . .

ASSESSMENT

Make a Record Sheet of your progress while writing poems in the last two steps. Have you used rhyme or repetition? What are your feelings about your own and others' poems?

— — — — — — — — — — — — — —

WRITING A STORY FOR YOUNG CHILDREN

9

Did you like bedtime stories when you were young? Perhaps some of them were about animals.

We ask you to think about writing for young children. It can be fun to have an audience to write for.

Mr Egbert Nosh

Once upon a time there was man called Egbert Nosh, Mr Egbert Nosh. Now Egbert Nosh lived in a house. The house stood in a road with other houses. Egbert liked his house best. He thought it was the best house in the road. Perhaps it was the best in all the world. That is until one day . . .

Well, one day Egbert Nosh went out for a walk. All of a sudden he heard footsteps behind him, quite heavy footsteps. He looked round to see who was following him. And what do you think he saw? Yes, there was his house walking down the road.

'This is ridiculous!' said Egbert.

'Why?' asked the House.

'Well, what do you think you are doing?'

'I'm going for a walk,' said the House.

'But houses don't go for walks,' said Egbert.

'This one does,' said the House.

'This is ridiculous,' said Egbert.

'So you keep saying,' said the House. 'Where are you going?'

'I'm going to . . . What does it matter to you where I'm going?'

'I want to come with you.'

'You can't come with me, you're not a dog. Go back home at once. This is ridiculous.'

'No.'

'Go home!'

'Not unless you do.'

'I'm not going back.'

'Then I shall stay out with you.'

'This is ridiculous,' said Egbert. He felt such a fool standing there in the middle of the road talking to a house. So he went back home. The House followed him. At home it sat down. Egbert opened the front door and went inside. He was very, very annoyed.

Now what could he do? He couldn't be followed by his house every time he wanted to go out; he had to go to the shops; he had to visit friends. Then an idea came to him.

Quietly, very quietly, he opened the front door. Even more quietly he shut it. Click. Then he ran down the path and into the road as fast as he could.

Down the road and round the corner was a bus-stop. If he could get there and on to a bus he would be away to the town. But what do you think he found when he got to the bus-stop? Yes, his House.

'This is ridiculous,' said Egbert. 'What are you doing here?'

'Waiting for a bus,' said the House.

'But houses don't go on buses.'

'This house does.'

Just then a bus drew up.

'Is this your house, sir?' asked the conductor.

'Yes,' said Egbert, 'but it's not with me.'

'Well, I'm afraid it's over regulation luggage size and it can't come on the bus.'

'Aha!' said Egbert. He jumped on the bus. The conductor rang the bell and the bus drove off.

But if Egbert had looked out of the back window . . . .

But he didn't. So he was rather surprised when in the middle of the town he saw his house, with a policeman standing by.

Egbert got off the bus. 'Is this your house?' asked the policeman.

'I'm afraid it is,' said Egbert.

'Sorry, sir,' said the policeman, 'but you can't park houses here, not on the double yellow lines. Take it away at once please.'

So Egbert opened the front door and went in. The House got up and walked back – very slowly.

Finish the story

▭▷ Finish the story yourself. Remember that an important aspect of telling or writing a story is to make the reader want to know what happens next. The following is a list of things that happen in the real 'Mr Egbert Nosh' story. You can either use them or make up an ending of your own.

Egbert tries to disguise himself.
He tries going out at night in the dark.
The House is not fooled.
The garage and dustbin follow as well.
In the end the House and Egbert have to come to an agreement.
What might that be?

Think about layout and punctuation

▭▷ In small groups, discuss the layout and punctuation of 'Mr Egbert Nosh'. When does a new *paragraph* start? Do you begin a new paragraph with each change of speaker? Look at the speech marks (inverted commas). Make up some rules for punctuating speech.

When do you need to use simple language in writing or speaking? Which book that you use at school has the hardest language? Why might you sometimes need to use difficult language? How can you learn to understand harder language than you read at present?

SPELL WELL

seek   creek   meek   reek

pale   Wales   whales   male   paler

quick   lick   sick   quickly   slick   tricky

FOOTNOTE

Paragraphs are often *indented*. What does that mean?

Write your own children's story

Try to make up a children's story of your own. Here are some suggestions.

1 In small groups, try to make up an imaginative story by contributing in turns. One starts and another continues, etc. If you get a good story, write it down and tell it to another group.

2 Put some objects on the table or desk in front of you, for example, a bunch of keys, a hand mirror, a pen. Now how fantastic can you get about each object? Remember in stories even houses can walk!

   The keys – What door do they unlock? What is behind the door? Is there a new world? Or are they the keys to a casket?

   A mirror – What is the world behind the mirror? Are things the wrong way round there? Do you keep bumping into yourself?

   A pen – This pen can write by itself. You just think hard and it works. How does it help at school? Who steals the pen? Where does it end up?

3 Play the 'what if' game. Look round where you are sitting and . . .

   What if the teacher's dog came in and started talking?

   What if a hole in the wall appeared and there was a stairway leading down?

   What if you looked out of the window and saw a flying saucer?

   Make up your own 'what ifs'.

4 Read some authors you enjoy and try to write a story as they do. Or use part of their story and add a new ending.
You might like to write another 'Egbert Nosh' story. What happens, for instance, if the house takes Egbert to the seaside when he is asleep?

5 List the things you think young children enjoy and then write a story about them, for example:
playing with a ball – this could become a magic ball.
playing hide and seek – a bear helps you to hide in his cave, but what then?
keeping pets – where does the cat go each night? Is there a secret world of cats?

6 Simplify a myth or legend from any culture.

ASSESSMENT

Make a Record Sheet of your progress while writing a children's story. What problems did you have while planning your story? Did you find it difficult coming up with an idea that would interest young children? Did you use direct speech in your story? When re-drafting your story, did you have to correct speech punctuation?

If you can, try out your story on an audience of young children. Write down their reaction in your Record Sheet.

— — — — — — — — — — — — — — —

FOOTNOTE

Try to write in a way that catches the child's interest. Compare these two openings. Which story do you think a child would like continued?

1 David had a little fluffy guinea pig called Cuddles. He cuddled it every day. It had a pretty face and red eyes. He was a good boy and fed it every day . . .

2 David said, 'Hello' to the monster. 'Hello, David,' said the monster. Then it ate him and belched. It was funny being in the monster's tummy when it belched. He was twirled round and round . . .

Naughtiness is a good subject providing naughty children get their come-uppance.

HOW WORDS WORK~
Proper nouns

10

Did you have many names in your stories? Names are special kinds of English words called proper nouns. They need special punctuation with capital letters.

There are other proper nouns as well as names.

⟹ Earlier we saw that nouns were the first and perhaps the most important words in English. Which are the nouns in this paragraph? Make a list of them.

Last Thursday I heard the first cuckoo of the year when I was staying with my aunt, Agatha Dixon, at her cottage in Dorset. I wrote to the 'Courier', the local paper for Tinton, my aunt's town, and they published my letter. Nobody has heard a cuckoo in February before.

Some nouns are called *proper nouns.* They always begin with a capital letter. Which are the proper nouns in the paragraph above?

⟹ Make a chart to show people how to decide which are proper nouns. You will need to work in groups of five or six, each person looking through a selection of books or magazines to decide the categories (types). The paragraph about the cuckoo will give you a start.

1 Days of the week: Thursday
2 People's names: Agatha Dixon
3 Counties: Dorset
4 Newspapers: Courier
5 Towns: Tinton

When you have found all the types you can, try to reduce the number of groups. For example, 'Names found on a map' would cover countries, towns, villages, rivers, seas, streets, etc.

FOOTNOTE

'Children are cleverer than adults think.'

Why would it be wrong in this sentence to think that *Children* is a proper noun?

What's in a name?

What's in a name? That which we call a rose
By any other name would smell as sweet;

(Romeo and Juliet)

⇨ On your own, write the answers to these questions. Each name you write must begin with a capital letter.

1 What is your first name?
2 Do you like it?
3 Is it really you?
4 If not, why not? What would you rather have been called?
5 If you have a middle name, what do you think of that?
6 Does your name have a diminutive, for example, Ted for Edward, Bet for Elizabeth?
7 If so, which do you prefer, the full name or the diminutive?
8 Do you have a nickname? If so, what is it?
9 Do you like it?
10 If you could choose a nickname, what would you call yourself?
11 What is your surname?
12 What do you think of it?
13 If you could change your surname by deed poll, what would you call yourself?
14 If you had a stage or a film name, what would you call yourself?
15 What would you regard as an upper-class name?
16 What would you regard as a working-class name?
17 Write down a name which you think sounds macho or tough.
18 Write down a name which you think sounds very feminine.
19 If you were the lead singer of a pop group, what would you like the group to be called?
20 What do you think of first names that are the same for both sexes (sometimes with a slight spelling difference)?
21 What is the most old-fashioned first name that you can think of?
22 Why were names invented in the first place?
23 If you had a pet, what would you call it?
24 If you could be seen and photographed with somebody famous, who would it be?

⇨ In small groups, read this letter from the *Weekend Guardian* and discuss it:

I recently caught an intercity train from Southampton to Weymouth. While standing in the 2nd class carriage I happened to notice a painting at each end of the carriage. They depicted scenes of the surrounding countryside and were signed Eddie Pond, 1977, a name I did not know. Anyway, they were pleasing to the eye and helped me to come to terms with the discomfort of standing. However their effect soon wore off and I decided to find a spare seat elsewhere in the train. This I failed to do and therefore resorted to a 1st class compartment. Once seated I happened again on similar scenes around the walls but this time they were signed by Edward Pond, 1977.

This set me thinking. If British Rail had chosen more famous artists for their trains (apologies to Eddie/Edward Pond) I wonder how they would have signed in the 2nd class carriages. Perhaps Lenny da Vinci, Vince Van Gogh or even Johnnie Constable?

Richard Dawton.

How would you sign a picture:

1 for your friends?
2 if it was going to Buckingham Palace? Can you think of some funny examples of how famous people might have signed their names in the 2nd class carriage?

A PERSONAL STORY FOR YOUR MAGAZINE

People usually write best when they have something they really want to tell others. Read Jonathan's story. It is printed just as written so there are some mistakes in it.

Think about sentence punctuation when you are reading the story.

The Hags – A True Story

Just around the corner from where I live there used to be a lovely big green field. My friend used to live right next to the field. But now she's living next to a big ugly housing estate.

First of all, this big sign went up beside my friend's house saying. 'Beazer Homes, changing the way Britain lives'. We weren't too pleased about this and we wondered what was happening. Two days later three massive JCB earth movers drove into the field and began to dig it up. By nightfall our field was a square of cloggy soil.

Over the next two years concrete mixers, gigantic lorries, more JCBs and hundreds of sweaty men transformed that one-time great play area into roads and houses, and left us a pathetic patch of grass to play on.

This patch of grass (or The Green) was the centre of the massive bout that was about to begin. For one day, myself, my friend and some other kids we'd made friends with, were playing Danish Long Ball on 'The Green', cheering each other on and ordinary things like that; when out of this house appeared this old woman of about fifty two. She ran onto the green and started shoving us off, she was actually pushing us off; she was claiming that it was her garden!

This totaly enraged us and when she went inside, we all rushed back on 'The Green' shouting abuse and chanting 'We shall not be moved!'

After a while we went home for our lunches.

When we returned we found she had planted flowers in 'her garden'. As soon as we came into view she came out and laid down these rules: We were not allowed to come onto her garden (our green) or her drive. Now we were not standing for that it was our green left there so us kids were not totally deprived of a play area. She thought she could just ponce onto what was ours long before she ever considered moving, and claim it was hers. So I spoke up and rang her bell. She answered the door and snapped, 'Get away from my house you yob!' 'Look here' I replied, 'This green is all we have left of an enormouse field, then the houses came and destroyed it, so you can't tell us to get off our property.' She just looked at me and slamed the door in our faces. So I rejoined everyone else on the green, kicking at her flowers. I was greeted with calls of, 'How did it go Jon?' 'What did you say Jon?' I told them briefly what happend and we continued to play on our green.

After about five minutes she 'Mrs Hag' yelled from her doorway, 'Get off my garden you hoodlums!' So I yelled back 'Get lost, you old cow!' She said she would get the police, none of us believed her and kept on the green. But sure enough a few hours later a police car rolled up the drive, we scampered off the green to the pavement and talked.

After an hour, the car left, the two policemen laughing.

It was getting towards tea time, so I went home for tea. I came back afterwards. I called for my friend, but she had to go to orchestra so I chatted to her younger brother about action against the Hags, (whose real names were the Hankies). We decided to take action immediately. It was still light outside, so we hid behind a hilly part of the green and waited. After the curtains had been drawn, we crept down to where their car was, a Rolls Royce Silver Shadow II (registration KPH 1) and let the tyres down. Then we picked up a massive lump of dry earth, and just as I was about to throw it over their fence into the back garden, Mr Hag jumped over the fence! As soon as we saw him we ran. He caught the younger lad, but I got away.

I could hear him asking Philip questions about me, he tried to bluff, but he spilled the beans. When he had gone, we got back together and talked about the preeceding events.

When I arrived home, Dad jumped down my throat and barked, 'I've just had a very angry woman on the phone saying that you've been causing trouble round her house. Now what's going on Jonathan?' I had to tell him and he grounded me for three weeks. During that time the Hags moved away thank God.

And there ended my scandal with the Hankies. But every time I'm outside and something goes wrong, I still get blamed for everything, but I just ignore them. I've learnt better than to answer back.

FOOTNOTE

Jonathan's presentation, punctuation and spelling are generally good. Notice:

1 His indenting for paragraphs – including one use of a one sentence paragraph.
2 His use of the exclamation mark.
3 His use of inverted commas.
4 His use of brackets.

Can you find any mistakes he has made?

The best way to learn to punctuate is to look how the experts do it in magazines and newspapers. Occasionally stop in this book and see how we have punctuated a page.

It is important that you get used to writing in sentences. Without correct sentence punctuation your reader may find your work difficult to understand. The best way to learn sentence punctuation is not by rules but by writing as much as possible. By and large Jonathan's sentences are good.

Jonathan's story is the first in a regular feature of his group's magazine called BAG (Boys and Girls). The title for the series of stories is: What Grown-ups Do to You.

▭ On your own, *either*:

1 contribute an article or story of your own to this series; *or*
2 imagine that the Hags saw his story. Write a letter from them to the magazine. They would probably have a very different view of what happened.

Role play

▭ In pairs, use the incident Jonathan describes to act out:

1 The telephone call from the Hankies to Jonathan's father.
2 The telephone call from the Hankies to the police.
3 The policeman's conversation after they'd failed to find Jonathan.
4 Jonathan's conversation with his father.

A sense of audience

Do you think Jonathan is writing for a particular type of audience? Which group of people do you think is not likely to be on his side?

Bias

Is Jonathan's language **biased**? (Does it lean you towards one point of view?) Look, for instance, at his title, his description of the housing estate, 'Mrs Hag'.

Fact or fiction?

Jonathan says it is a true story. Do you believe him? Can you find any evidence?

HOW TO INTERVIEW SOMEONE

12

In this Step we ask you to do a spot of interviewing. It may look easy on television but it takes skill to bring people to talk about themselves in an interesting way.

Read the following two interviews prepared by Annabel. Then read what she has to say about the differences between the two interviews.

Interview with a young person

I sat down opposite a small, black-haired boy with dark eyes. His name was Andrew James Gedge and he was fourteen years old. He looked a bit worried when he saw the pages of questions I had to ask him, but he managed to smile. We sat there for a few seconds wondering who was going to be the first one to ask a question. Finally I gave in and started.

'Have you any brothers or sisters?' I asked him.

'Yer, I've got one brother Chris, and a sister, Liz,' he says, turning up his nose.

I went on to find out that he lives in Bluntisham and supports Everton. He likes Queen but can't stand Bros. Andrew has one dog, one cat, eight hamsters, two guinea pigs and countless goldfish.

'What really irritates you?' I ask.

'Interviewers,' is his reply.

Well, that's charming, isn't it!

He claims that the bravest thing he ever has done is rescue his hamster from the cat. Andrew likes playing squash and fishing.

'What would your ideal girl look like?' I ask. He's thinking very hard about this one; he has a serious frown on his face.

'Well, em, I suppose she would have to be tall and have blonde or brown hair. She would have to have a good personality of course,' he answers.

He says the most useless present he has ever received was a duck pencil sharpener, which was from his brother Chris.

'I don't think I'm a very outgoing person, I'm not very loud,' he says.

Stephen, Andrew's friend, seems to think this is funny and starts laughing. According to him Andrew's always 'mouthing off'.

Finally I ask him what his favourite food is. He says he likes Italian food.

Now it's my turn to be interrogated by him.

Interview with an older person

Phylis May Staples was born on the 10th of November, 1919 in South East London. She has two sisters and one brother. According to Phylis life was different when she was young; people went at a slower pace. Nowadays everyone rushes everywhere and nobody has time to stay and talk.

Phylis (or Phyl as her friends call her) didn't like school. She says it was very strict. She left school when she was fourteen and got a job packing tea. But that was only for a few months. Soon after that she got a job in printing where she met her husband, Stanley Staples. (He died five years ago.) They were soon married and had two daughters Pamela and Norma. Phylis moved to Cambridgeshire from London 18 years ago to be with her two daughters.

Her ideal holiday would be a fortnight in the Isle of Wight. She has been going there for the past 30 years and has no desire to travel abroad.

If Phyl won a million pounds she says she would use it to pay off her children's mortgages and split the rest among her four grandchildren.

Cheeky children and people who moan a lot irritate her a lot. Phylis enjoys gardening but unfortunately doesn't have a garden of her own.

She didn't have any ambitions when she was young. She says children weren't as ambitious as they are nowadays. Phylis is happy that women now have more opportunities at work. She says her mum was always at home and a lot less women went to work when she was younger. She thinks education is a lot better these days and the children know a lot more than she did.

She has never had a useless present because she always tells people what she wants for her birthday or Christmas. Phylis enjoys sight-seeing and walking in the country.

Differences between the two interviews

I felt a lot more relaxed interviewing someone of my own age than someone older. My questions were slightly different in the two interviews. When I interviewed the older person most of my questions seemed to be about the past because they had done more things than the younger person. But with the younger person the questions were aimed at the future because he has his whole life ahead of him, whereas the older person doesn't. I thought it was a lot more interesting interviewing the older person because they had a lot more to say and they had done a lot more things in their life than the younger person.

Annabel

Prepare your questions and make notes

Before you begin an interview, you have to prepare the questions you are going to ask. Annabel has obviously prepared her questions well.

▭ Make a list of the questions Annabel has asked each person. Now add your own questions you would like to ask an old and a young person. Write your questions out in full or make *notes* like this:

> Pet hate
> Worst fear
> Happiest day

▭ Now interview two people and make notes at your interview. Don't try to write down everything they say. Make notes like this:

> People who smoke
> Locked in lav with spiders
> Day I won competition

Now write up your interviews the way Annabel has done.

FOOTNOTE

Annabel has written down her first interview in the present time (*present tense*). She writes:

> Stephen *seems* to think this is funny. (*present tense*)
> *instead of*
> Stephen *seemed* to think this was funny. (past tense)

You can use either but don't mix up both in one interview. Check with your teacher when you are in the first draft stage.

ASSESSMENT

Prepare a Record Sheet of your progress while doing the interviews. You should have a lot to report under the heading: 'The preparation'. It would probably be best to have two headings after 'Planning the task': 'The interviews' and 'Writing up the interviews'. Then go on to 'Assessment', etc.

DEFINITIONS ~ WHAT WORDS MEAN

13

It is now time to take a look at definitions or what words mean. You will need to know about adjectives to do your own definitions – another of our Words at Work.

'When I use a word,' Humpty Dumpty said, 'it means just what I choose it to mean – neither more nor less.'

Lewis Carroll

What kind of a mess would we get into if we were all like Humpty Dumpty?

Dictionaries can help you to find out how to spell words but their main job is to tell you what words mean.

⇨ Here are ten dictionary definitions. Decide what word is being defined in each case:

Clue – They are all nouns and are in alphabetical order.

1 Woman on her wedding day
2 Prison of wire or bars, especially for birds and animals
3 The under surface of the top of a room
4 A narrow trench for draining off water
5 Members of a household
6 Four-legged animal with a very long neck and legs
7 Man on his wedding day
8 An error or blunder
9 Protective covering for injured eye
10 Burrowing mammal related to the hare

Write your own definitions

⇨ Some of the simplest words are the hardest to define. Try making definitions for these:

cat dog bear elephant fox hen pig

Try reading some of your definitions to a partner. Can he or she guess them all? Which parts of your definition were most useful?

The Definition Game

In small groups   4–6 players.

You will need small squares of paper and a dictionary. Each player takes it in turn to find a word in the dictionary that she or he thinks nobody will know the meaning of. Read out the word to check that no one knows the real meaning. The person with the dictionary then copies down the definition while the others make up a definition for the word – yes, just like Humpty Dumpty. All definitions are then collected. The person with the dictionary reads out all the definitions on the pieces of paper including his or her own. The rest of the players take it in turn to guess the true definition.

Scoring

The player with the dictionary scores 1 point if nobody guesses the true definition. Each of the other players gains a point each time someone guesses his or her false definition as the true one.

The dictionary is passed to the next player. The game ends when someone has scored 6 points.

Note 1

The skill is to make your false definition sound like a true one. For example, which of these is the true definition of 'guano'?

1 a board game for six players?
2 a small fish found only in the Indian Ocean?
3 the droppings of sea birds used for fertilizer?
4 a goblin with long legs?

Look up the definition before you begin the game.

Note 2

You can save time if each player looks up some definitions before the game starts.

When a definition is not enough

LOST CAT

It is a four-legged domestic furry animal. If found, please return to Aziz Jeffrey
Tel : 69301   Reward

Aziz might have several phone calls, but no caller would be sure if she or he had found the cat.

The definition defines the type of animal – a cat. It does not describe a particular cat.

⟹ Choose one of these dogs and make a lost notice for it.

In pairs, exchange notices with a partner. Is there any doubt which dog he or she is describing?

Decide which words were most helpful. They will probably have been words like: small, large, fierce, sad, long-eared, fat, thin, white, black.

These are all describing words. They are *adjectives.*

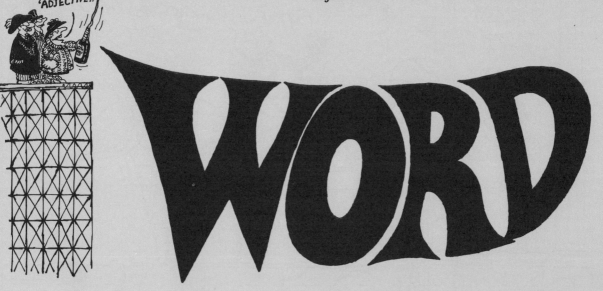

The Adjective Game

In small groups   5–6 players
Player A chooses a noun – dog, house, grandad, book, etc. The players then have five seconds each to name an adjective for the noun. Each round stops when a player fails to think of an adjective, repeats an adjective used already, says an adjective of the same meaning, or chooses an adjective that means the opposite of one already used. You must not contradict or repeat. For example:

PIG – fat, dirty, smelly, fierce, old, *filthy*
Filthy stops the round and the player loses a point; its meaning is too near to *dirty.*

CAR – black, shiny, new, big, fast, noisy, sleek, *old*
Old stops the round because it contradicts *new.*

Note   Each adjective must make sense as a description of the noun. For instance, people describe cars as *pretty, amazing,* even *heavenly,* but you could not call a car *brave* or *crafty.*

The Invention of Adjectives

Adjectives were invented in Roman times by a slave called Yecti. Every week his master drove a herd of cows to be sold at the market. They were herded into a large pen and buyers crowded round to select the cow they wanted. Before a buyer decided which cow he wanted Yecti had to climb into the cow-pen and touch each one until the buyer signalled that it was the one he had decided on. It was dangerous work and Yecti was often butted unconscious or trampled on.

One night before the market Yecti took some paint and while the cows were asleep he made a different sign for each one. Then he painted the same signs on a board.

The next day at the market the buyers were able to point to the sign on the board to show which cow they wanted. This saved Yecti from further injury and soon he became quite famous. You would often hear Romans trying to describe something telling each other to add some Yectis.

Adjectives soon took off in a big way – colours, sizes, shapes, for instance, had been invented by the time of Yecti's death in 39 BC.

If you don't think this story is true, then write the 'real' one about the invention of adjectives. If you do think it's true, then don't tell anyone!

SPELL WELL

seal steal meal real congeal peal

cough dough enough bough rough
tough

sight might insight tight nightly

FROM SPOKEN TO WRITTEN WORDS ~ A transcription

14

How do people actually speak? How is it different from written down sentences? Have you ever tried tape-recording? Here we look at Lee telling a story to his class. The story was recorded and written down just as Lee said it. This is called a *transcription*.

And continuing our study of Words at Work we take a look at pronouns and the important job they do.

No, it's straight up, this is. Just listen. Right. The next door . . . I won't say their names . . . they don't like us. And they don't like this dog . . . our dog . . . What? It's called Fido . . . you only asked because you knew . . . it's all true, I'm telling you. So they've got this rabbit, see er . . . shut up . . . the neighbours' rabbit. Well, we were sitting watching telly . . . I can't remember . . . let me get on . . . and in comes Fido . . . through the flap with their rabbit . . . it was all covered in clag . . . you know . . . muck . . . dead, yea, it was dead all right . . . so we didn't know what to do . . . I mean we couldn't go and tell them . . . so in the end we washed it in the bath and Mum blow-dried it and then I made its ears stick up . . . and . . . shut up . . . it's true . . . with gel . . . hair gel . . . and then I took it back when it was dark . . . they were out . . . anyway there were no lights on . . . I stuck it back in its cage . . . made it sit up so it looked alive . . . I had to spread its legs out . . . they'll think it had like a heart attack or something . . . well . . . that's what we thought . . . er . . . then what . . . well two days later Mrs Carnell . . . forget that . . . the neighbour meets my Mum . . . well my Mum was just setting off . . . for work and this woman was setting out her rubbish bag and she had this box as well . . . and in the box was this dead rabbit . . . oh dear, has your rabbit died, Mrs C . . . well I'm not in the habit of putting live rabbits in dustbins . . . she was always sort of snotty like that . . . then she says . . . has your Lee been up to something . . . she never liked me . . . up to what says Mum . . . it's a very funny thing . . . our rabbit died three days ago and we buried it and then two days later it was back in its cage . . . now who would do a thing like that . . . only a mental person . . . so we're putting it in the bin this time . . . well, I'm sure my Lee wouldn't do a thing like that . . . well somebody did . . . my Mum said cheerio and came in . . . course it's true . . . I wouldn't make it up . . . no way.

▭ In small groups, discuss the story. How do you know that this is a spoken rather than a written story? On several occasions the class interrupt Lee asking questions or commenting on his story. What questions do they ask? How can you tell that Lee is having trouble making the class believe his story? Do you believe it?

Turn the transcript into a written story

▭ On your own, make a written version of Lee's story. You will be able to miss out some of the things he says, but keep in the conversation between Lee's Mum and the neighbour, Mrs Carnell. Punctuate it correctly. In a transcription you can use dots to show the pauses, but in a story you will need sentence punctuation. You will also need speech punctuation for the conversation. Make sure you do it correctly.

▭ Make a short newspaper article from Lee's story entitled:

Try to make it as dramatic as possible. You will have interviewed Mrs Carnell, the neighbour. But, of course, you won't know Lee's side of the story.

▭ Write four to six lines about the differences in language shown in the three pieces: the transcript, the written version and the newspaper article. Why is each different from the others?

Use a tape recorder

If you can use a tape recorder, you can tell each other stories and tape them. Then write them in transcript. You might have a competition for the most far-fetched story.

'The Bunny They Couldn't Bury'

SPELL WELL

trail mail sail hail tail failure

money lone phoney honest tone

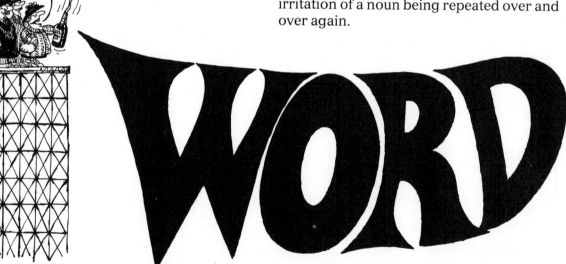

A little word of importance – pronouns

Read this paragraph:

Dejian walked home with Saila from school. Saila didn't want Dejian to but Dejian did it all the same. Dejian asked Saila if Saila would come to Angie's party with Dejian. Dejian had asked Saila a hundred times that week. In the end Saila told Dejian that if Dejian couldn't take 'no' for an answer Saila would ask Dejian's teacher to keep Dejian in until Saila got quickly home to Saila's house.

▭▷ Write this out as you think it should be written. In doing so you will be substituting words for nouns – you will be using *pronouns*.

A pronoun's job in a sentence is to avoid the irritation of a noun being repeated over and over again.

▭▷ Use books to compile a list of pronouns. Remember that you are looking for words that stand in place of nouns. Here is a start:

  she he . . .

You can check in a dictionary. They will be marked *pron* or *pronoun*.

THE LANGUAGE OF FORMS AND LETTERS

15

Do your parents complain about filling in forms? You will learn why as you grow up. All the more reason to start looking at the language of forms now.

We take our first look at letters.

The Step ends with a survey on shopping.

Filling in forms

Christmas is coming. Your most urgent need is for money. You go to your local Post Office to withdraw some. You hand in your Savings Book and you are handed this form or you look for it on display.

ORDINARY ACCOUNT

WITHDRAWAL ON DEMAND

NATIONAL SAVINGS

Date	Month	Year 19

Account number

Amount
£   p

Amount in words _____

Full names **M** _____
(CAPITAL letters) Enter Mr, Mrs, Miss or Ms

Address _____

_____ Postcode _____

Please sign in the presence of the paying officer, who may ask for evidence of identity.
I acknowledge receipt of the above amount.

Signature

For post office use

3

Balance after this withdrawal   £   p

Please check

(a) You have seen the signature written
(b) Signature and account number same as book
(c) Book security features in order
(d) Last deposit transaction in order
(e) Entry made in book
(f) Balance entered above
(g) Book retained if required to

All items attended to

Date stamp

....
Initials

DNS 10 (88/01)
HMSO Dd4196 30m 9830 1/88

NB: At the Post Office the pink form is the withdrawal form and the blue one is the deposit form (putting money in).

Your teacher will give you a form. *Do not mark this book in any way.*

Date: Fill this in in figures though you can use three letters for the month e.g. DEC.

Account number: Make one up. Put a figure in each of the nine spaces.

Amount: Fill in the figures, putting pounds first.

Amount in words: Fill in like this – EIGHTEEN POUNDS FIFTY PENCE.

Full Names: USE CAPITAL LETTERS OR BLOCK CAPITALS. Check the list below that you can write these properly:
A B C D E F G H I J K L M N O P
Q R S T V U W X Y Z

Address: Write in your full address in capital letters.

Postcode: Learn your post code if you don't know it.

Signature: Write your normal signature.

For post office use: Put nothing in this section of the form.

When you have made your withdrawal you buy some stamps for your Christmas cards. Last year you missed some people out. This year you are going to make a list in alphabetical order.

⟹ Make a list now of those you will post including friends and relatives. You may need to check the postal codes but for this exercise you can make them up.

This is how you address an envelope:

MR & MRS J T EDLEY
BURNHAM CROFT
3 MAIN STREET
WORKINGTON
CUMBRIA
CA 12 4 NQ

Capital letters will help the postman. Note that no punctuation is needed.

Make an address book

⟹ Make an address book by putting A, B, C, etc, at the top of the pages of a note book (one letter per page) – or else cut down the edge like a bought address book. Fill in the addresses of your friends and relatives.

⟹ You decide to buy one of the T-shirts (opposite) for your sister or brother. Fill in the form your teacher will give you. *Do not mark this book in any way.*

STEP THIS WAY FOR ALL YOUR ESSENTIAL WINTER WEARABLES!

Has your wardrobe got that tired look? Our togs style-Viewers, do you a clothes-lift? here at fashion-ious *Smash Hits* got the means to ur gear to rights! s. Marvel at the d of exclusive ! Choose from the rt of your own g-room! "Meet" mash Hits gue and banish sartorial blues for Soopah!

Gurreat white short-sleeved T-shirt decorated back and sleeve with "motifs" as a star! A ! Some writing that 'Smash Hits Poll ners' Party '89'! A at **£7.25!**

B Fantastic white T-shirt with long sleeves for those nippy winter morns! It's got the exclusive Smash Hits Poll winners design on it too, plus more '89s a-twirling down the lengthy sleeve! And it's only **£9.50!**

C "Trendy" black hooded T-shirt with short sleeves! And it, too, sports the Smash Hits star and circle and reams of guff about the '89 Poll Winners' Party! At **£11.00**, it's a complete "steal"!

D Handy so-called "boom-bags" in groovy mauve and fluorescent yellow! They've got *Smash Hits* written on them! And you can put lots of stuff in them! You'd be a goat to miss out when they're only **£7.75!**

w to get hold of the ed items. . .
mplete the easy-to-fill-in n and put it in an envelope panied by a cheque or order (made payable to Merchandising S/H) for the mount.
nd it all off to **PO Box 50,** w, Essex CM17 ODZ. it for 28 days until the whole irls onto your mat! en it all up, don the essential-nclosed and – hey presto! – in "demand"

EASY-TO-FILL COUPON

● Put the number of items you want in the little boxes provided.

A White short-sleeved T-shirt £7.25
☐ Med ☐ Large ☐ Extra large

B White long-sleeved T-shirt £9.50
☐ (one size only)

C Black hooded T-shirt £11.00
☐ (one size only)

D "Boom-bag" £7.75
☐ Mauve ☐ Fluorescent yellow

● I enclose a cheque/postal order made payable to Event Merchandising S/H for .... to cover the cost of all the items.

MY NAME IS ....

MY ADDRESS IS ....

....

....

● Fill in this coupon and send it to: **PO Box 50, Harlow, Essex CM17 ODZ.** Allow 28 days for delivery. All prices include postage and packing.

Write a friendly note

People love to receive notes on their Christmas cards. Here is a note from Brian to his grandmother:

To Grandma,

MERRY CHRISTMAS

Hope you are well. I have grown 3 inches this year. Photo enclosed. I won a tennis trophy at school. I've also become very keen on gardening and work in the school greenhouse. My sunflowers grew 8 feet this year !

love Brian

A note on a Christmas card does not have to be as formal as a letter. Every thought does not have to be a complete sentence. You do not have to worry about paragraphs.

⟹ Write these notes that could go on Christmas cards:

1 One that could go on a card to a relative who has been ill.
2 One that could go on a card to someone you would like to be friendly with again.
3 One to your favourite relation.

Setting out a letter

Look at this letter that was sent to the editor of a local newspaper.

Notice how the letter is set out on the page. Look at other letters in newspapers and magazines to see how this is done. Susan has written her letter in two paragraphs. Each paragraph has a *topic sentence* which explains the main point of the paragraph. Pick out the topic sentences in Susan's paragraphs.

27 Prior Lane,
Garston,
Lancaster.
LA18 9JM

30th November 1990

Dear Editor,

I think it would be a good idea if there was not so much pressure to buy things at Christmas. The adverts start on TV months before December the 25th. My friends and I worry because we don't have enough pocket money to buy expensive presents for everyone.

My Dad says that Christmas used to be much nicer than it is now. People didn't start to shop for presents until just before Christmas. Sometimes they even made things for each other. And Christmas Day was a really nice time for relatives and neighbours to be together. I wonder what has happened to the 'spirit' of Christmas?

Yours sincerely,

Susan Harris

Susan Harris

Write your own letters

▭ Your father or mother is annoyed very much by young carol singers. These children, aged about seven, keep knocking on your door, singing one verse of a carol badly and asking for money. You decide to write to the local paper about the nuisance. You write the letter to the following plan (plan A on page 85). If you are not sure about how to set out a letter, look back at Susan's letter on page 83.

Check any spellings you are unsure of in your dictionary. You may like to do two drafts and pick the best.

▭ Your mother insists that you write to Aunt Edna thanking her for the pink socks she sent you. Write the letter to plan B on page 85.

ASSESSMENT

Prepare a Record Sheet of your progress while writing the letters in this Step. Which did you find easier to write: a formal or informal letter? Which letter took the most preparation?

A

Address and
Date

Dear Sir,

Paragraph One: State what has been happening as outlined above.

Paragraph Two: Ask if the children's parents know what they are doing.

Paragraph Three: Point out the dangers of young children going round knocking on strange doors in the dark.

Paragraph Four: Urge other householders not to give money to these children but to give it to charity instead.

Yours faithfully,

Signature

B

Address and
Date

Dear Aunt Edna,

Paragraph One: Say how you enjoyed your present which you wore to a party. Say no one else gave you pink socks.

Paragraph Two: Tell her something about what you have done at Christmas.

Paragraph Three: Give her some news of the family.

Paragraph Four: Ask after her health and say you hope to see her in the New Year. Wish her a happy New Year.

Sign off:

Love

A shopping survey

While you are out Christmas shopping you are asked to answer a survey.
Here it is:

Age?
Sex?
Occupation?
How did you get to the shopping area?
Which street or centre do you prefer to shop in?
Your favourite shop?
How many presents do you hope to get for people?
What worries you most about Christmas shopping?
Is there anything you can't get locally?
Have you had to queue anywhere? If so, where?
Do you expect to spend more than you want to?
Will you be in debt by the end of the month?
Is Christmas too commercialised?
Which charity do you give to at Christmas time?
What singles have you bought or expect to buy?
What albums have you bought or expect to buy?
What toiletries have you bought or expect to buy?
What toys have you bought or expect to buy?
What books have you bought or expect to buy?
What consumables (things you eat) have you bought or expect to buy?

⇨ Working in pairs, write this out and
answer it. *Do not mark this book.*

⇨ Write a short piece for your school
magazine or newspaper based on this
survey called: 'The Perils and Pleasures of
Christmas Shopping.'

THE LANGUAGE OF SELLING

16

Advertising affects all our lives more than we realise. The more you know about advertising, the more control you will have over your life.

Here we look at past and present advertising from magazines to radio.

Looking at advertisements

▭ In small groups, look at these six advertisements from a local paper.

1 Why are they not written in sentences? For example, why is the last one not written:

'I have a large electronic organ for sale, which is in beautiful condition. I'm sure that the first person to see it will buy.'?

2 What does o.n.o. and K.C. registered mean?

Raleigh Cameo girl's bicycle, needs new tyres (not used for ages) otherwise all right. £50 o.n.o. 3 George St.

American Cocker Spaniel 8 months old male, black and white, K.C. registered, fully inoculated. Tel: 61556

Royal Python with all necessary equipment. £200. Safe quiet easy care. 3ft fully grown. Serious offers only. Tel: 300484

Ski Jacket small size, never been worn, reversible, bright yellow or rainbow colours. £25 Tel: 67439

Piano Tuition for beginners. Playing the piano is fun. Please phone 51923 evenings

Farsina large electronic organ. Beautiful condition. First to see will buy. £200 o.n.o. Tel: 300028

3 The longest advert is for the python. Why has the owner used more words? How is he or she trying to re-assure buyers? Why does the ad say 'Serious offers only'?

4 How could you cut down the bike and the organ adverts?

⮕ On your own, Make these into advertisements, using only the important information for your purpose. If the adverts
cost 10p per word or number (e.g. £10), how
much would your advert cost?

1 My rabbit has died and I do not want
another so I wish to sell his cage, which is
large and has two doors. I think it is
worth £10 but I might accept a little less.

2 I am emigrating to Australia and I cannot
take my dog, Spot, who is a large bull
terrier. I want to find him a good home, so
I am willing to sell him for just £80, which
is only half of what he cost me a year ago.

⮕ Make your own small advertisements,
giving a telephone number as in the examples. Collect and re-distribute the adverts at
random round the groups. Which adverts
are the best?

Role play: using the telephone

Choose one of the adverts and pretend to
telephone the number. The person who
wrote the advert answers the phone. You
then negotiate a sale and a meeting. You act
out the meeting.

SPELL WELL

practice   nice   ice-cream   office   invoice

those   whose   chose   lose   closet

mountain   count   counterfeit   bounty

Did you understand the message?

So far we have only looked at the do-it-yourself type of advert that is looking for just one buyer. Here and on page 90 are some adverts that intend to sell to many people.

➡ In small groups, make notes on the ways these adverts try to sell.

Consider what use they make of:

1 Different-sized type
2 Illustrations
3 Free offers

Decide which type of person each advertisement is aimed at.
Do you think the advertisers have found the right language for the type of person? Find examples in each case.

➡ In pairs, design an advert of your own for a real product or one you have invented. You may use coloured letters or illustrations (a face, for instance) cut out of old magazines. Try to make the language fit the customer.

For young people aged 5 – 15
ACTION HOLIDAYS
speak louder than words!

Phone: (0565) 54775 for Free Colour Brochure
Action Holidays, Windrush, Bexton Lane, Knutsford, Cheshire WA16 9BP

27 CHILDREN KILLED OR SERIOUSLY INJURED TODAY

As statistics show, when children travel without proper protection it can have very serious consequences.

The fact that accidents happen at all is tragic. These figures could be significantly reduced simply by making sure that all children are properly secured in the first place.

That's why at Britax we've designed a range of child seats, harnesses and adult seat belts to take care of you and your family. They're easy to use and all provide the reassurance you need.

So make certain your child travels in a Britax car seat because statistics don't always happen to other people.

Britax

Britax, 1 Churchill Way West, Andover, Hampshire SP10 3UW. Tel: 0264 333343.
a BSG international plc company

Beautiful Skin
— by Ella Baché Paris —

If you have tried everything and still have **SPOTS, BLEMISHES, BLACKHEADS, OPEN PORES, DRY AND SENSITIVE SKIN, WRINKLES,** write to us for a FREE Booklet and we'll show you how it is easily done to have that clear complexion you've always wanted. You'll be very glad to have found us.
Send s.a.e. to:
Consulting Beautician,
Ella Baché
5 Harrington Road,
London SW7 3ES.
01-584 8746/7

HOLY BATSHIRTS!

Well, actually they're totally hole free Batshirts and they're *the* thing to cover your chest with this summer hol.

With the new *Batman* movie out on August 11, there's gonna be a host of **amazing** Bat goodies around. But these here shirts, by LCI, are *the* official ones!

There are eleven designs, ranging from the Batman logo, to the manic Joker spouting words of wisdom like 'You can't make an omelette without breaking some eggs' — the shirt for Edwina Currie, perhaps?

You can get hold of the shirts for around £7.99 from Virgin Record shops and places like Top Shop and Hennes. Or you could answer an easy question and win one of the ten we've got to give away.

Just tell us the name of the famous actor who plays the Joker in the new Batman film and send answers to: GIRL/Holy Batshirts, 27th Floor, King's Reach Tower, Stamford Street, London SE1 9LS.

JOKES

FREE

CATALOGUE

Packed with practical jokes, special pop and football bargains. Whoopee cushion, black face soap, water bombs, joke teeth, slime spiders, snakes, magic ink, itching powder, soap sweets, joke tea bags, skeletons, volcanic sugar, wet jokes, bang jokes, magic tricks, masks, prankster tricks to play on friends and enemies.

(Joke Club details big savings, free badge and gift). Over 500 jokes to choose from, many under 20p also pop and football scarves, hats, keyrings, rosettes, badges, sweatbands, bracelets, picture combs and lots more. Send 2nd class stamp with your name and address for bumper catalogue and free gift to:

**JOKE SHOP
BY POST**

(Dept. KET)
167 Winchester Road,
Bristol BS4 3NJ

Advertising in the past

Advertising has changed almost beyond recognition in the last 100 years.

Look at 'Boardie Willie'. What is he advertising? Why have he and his sandwich-board become so out-of-date?

▭ Imagine that Bella Pateman is the lead singer in a pop group whose new single has just hit number 1 in the charts. Design an advertisement for a concert that the group will be giving in your town. Your ad will probably be illustrated and in colour.

Then read 'Important to all to have good overcoats', which is from the *Grantham Journal*, 17 November 1855 (page 92).

▭ How might W. Brice advertise in a modern newspaper? Make a full page advertisement for him. Use some of the ideas presented in the Grantham Journal advert, but put them in up-to-date language. Your ad will probably be illustrated.

Important to all to have good overcoats

The winter's approaching, the year's in its fall.
A few words we will give worth the notice of all;
Economise justly, wherever you can,
If you want to grow rich, is an excellent plan.
To buy good things at a low price
For the clothing you want do purchase of Brice;
'Tis the richest apparel that ever was made
At prices far less than elsewhere in the trade.
While the cut, and the style, and the exquisite fit,
A gentleman's taste cannot fail to hit.
Dress well and save money you easily can,
And to prove it a fact W. Brice is the man;
Now all who would show their health they respect,
Should a suitable change at Brice's wardrobe select.
We shall soon have days foggy, wet, chilly and damp
Rare time for sore throats, rheumatic and cramp.
And a great many more very terrible ills,
Not least among which are doctor's long bills.
This may all be avoided and cheaply that is clear,
By suiting your dress to the time of the year;
And surely 'tis better the tailor to pay,
Than on physic your cash to be throwing away.
Brice's gorgeous display of fashion's the last,
'Tis a glorious sight that cannot be surpassed.
The prices the lowest of any yet known,
Indeed for small price, Brice's all and alone.
Unequalled for quality, workmanship, and well-made,
Brice's youths and men's clothing are the best in the trade.
Then to Brice's great wardrobe repair,
Health, wealth, taste and fashion are waiting you there.

THIS ESTABLISHMENT HAS LONG BEEN
CELEBRATED FOR POSSESSING
A STOCK UNPARALLELED IN EXTENT, MATCHLESS
IN STYLE, AND
UNEQUALLED FOR CHEAPNESS, AT PRICES THAT
WILL ASTONISH YOU.

LIBERAL DISCOUNT FOR CASH

W. BRICE, TAILOR, HATTER, HOSIER, AND GENERAL
OUTFITTER
NO 1, and 2 North Parade, Grantham

A radio advert

Advertising on radio is expensive. The advert that follows lasts thirty
seconds.

▭ In small groups make a radio advert for any product you wish. You
will need to plan and practise carefully before you record your advert.
Remember all you have is sound – no pictures, no colour, no different-sized
type. But you can vary your voices and use as many sounds as you like.
Before you begin your own advert, practise this advert, using sound effects.

MV is a male voice – decide which type of voice best suits your advert.
FV would be a female voice.
FX is sound effects.
Most adverts will have more than one voice.

FX (Running footsteps, panting)
MV It's no good running, Rebecca.
FX (Footsteps cease – still panting)
MV You know you're too late. The shops are all shut. You've done it again,
     haven't you?
FX (Clanging sound)
MV Yes, that's right. You've dropped another clanger. Whose birthday is it
     tomorrow? Your Mum's this time. No card and no present.
FX (Clanging sound)
MV I'm right, aren't I?
FX (Plodding footsteps going away)
MV No, stay, Rebecca. You're in luck. There is one shop still open. Do you
     know Abdullah's, Rebecca? There's a branch in your town and it's open
     from eight till late every weekday with a huge selection of cards and
     presents for all people on all occasions.
FX (Running footsteps, panting)
MV Rebecca, stop.
FX (Footsteps and panting cease)
MV No need to hurry. Abdullah's is open from eight till late. Remember
     eight till late.
FX (Footsteps slow)
MV That's right, Rebecca. Plenty of time. Think of what to buy as you go.
     You're sure to find what you want at Abdullah's.

ASSESSMENT

Make a Record Sheet of your progress in
writing adverts throughout this step.

— — — — — — — — — — — — — — — —

CHARACTERS IN A STORY

17

In this Step we think about characters in a story. Your stories will be good if you have interesting characters in them.

The interest in 'William's Version' by Jan Mark is not so much what happens, but in the character of William.

William's Version

William and Granny were left to entertain each other for an hour while William's mother went to the clinic.

'Sing to me,' said William.

'Granny's too old to sing,' said Granny.

'I'll sing to you, then,' said William. William only knew one song. He had forgotten the words and the tune, but he sang it several times, anyway.

'Shall we do something else now?' said Granny.

'Tell me a story,' said William. 'Tell me about the wolf.'

'Red Riding Hood?'

'No, not *that* wolf, the other wolf.'

'Peter and the wolf?' said Granny.

'Mummy's going to have a baby,' said William.

'I know,' said Granny.

William looked suspicious.

'How do you know?'

'Well...she told me. And it shows, doesn't it?'

'The lady down the road had a baby. It looks like a pig,' said William. He counted on his fingers. 'Three babies looks like three pigs.'

'Ah,' said Granny. 'Once upon a time there were three little pigs. Their names were –'

'They didn't have names,' said William.

'Yes they did. The first pig was called –'

'Pigs don't have names.'

'Some do. These pigs had names.'

'No they didn't.' William slid off Granny's lap and went to open the corner cupboard by the fireplace. Old magazines cascaded out as old magazines do when they have been flung into a cupboard and the door slammed shut. He rooted among them until he found a little book covered with brown paper, climbed into the cupboard, opened the book, closed it and climbed out again. 'They didn't have names,' he said.

'I didn't know you could read,' said Granny, properly impressed.

'C – A – T, wheelbarrow,' said William.

'Is that the book Mummy reads to you out of?'

'It's my book,' said William.

'But it's the one Mummy reads?'

'If she says please,' said William.

'Well, that's Mummy's story, then. My pigs have names.'

'They're the wrong pigs.' William was not open to negotiation. 'I don't want them in this story.'

'Can't we have different pigs this time?'

'No. They won't know what to do.'

'Once upon a time,' said Granny, 'there were three little pigs who lived with their mother.'

'Their mother was dead,' said William.

'Oh, I'm sure she wasn't,' said Granny.

'She was dead. You make bacon out of dead pigs. She got eaten for breakfast and they threw the rind out for the birds.'

'So the three little pigs had to find homes for themselves.'

'No.' William consulted his book. 'They had to build little houses.'

'I'm just coming to that.'

'You said they had to *find* homes. They didn't *find* them.'

'The first little pig walked along for a bit until he met a man with a load of hay.'

'It was a lady.'

'A lady with a load of hay?'

'NO! It was a lady-pig. You said *he.*'

'I thought all the pigs were little boy-pigs,' said Granny.

'It says lady-pig here,' said William. 'It says the lady-pig went for a walk and met a man with a load of hay.'

'So the lady-pig,' said Granny, 'said to the man, "May I have some of that hay to build a house?" and the man said, "Yes." Is that right?'

'Yes,' said William. 'You know that baby?'

'What baby?'

'The one Mummy's going to have. Will that baby have shoes on when it comes out?'

'I don't think so,' said Granny.

'It will have cold feet,' said William.

'Oh, no,' said Granny. 'Mummy will wrap it up in a soft shawl, all snug.'

'I don't *mind* if it has cold feet,' William explained. 'Go on about the lady-pig.'

'So the little lady-pig took the hay and built a little house. Soon the wolf came along and the wolf said – '

'You didn't tell where the wolf lived.'

'I don't know where the wolf lived.'

'15 Tennyson Avenue, next to the bomb-site,' said William.

'I bet it doesn't say that in the book,' said Granny, with spirit.

'Yes it does.'

'Let me see, then.'

William folded himself up with his back to Granny, and pushed the book up under his pullover.

'*I* don't think it says that in the book,' said Granny.

'It's in ever so small words,' said William.

'So the wolf said, "Little pig, little pig, let me come in," and the little pig answered, "No". So the wolf said, "Then I'll huff and I'll puff and I'll blow your house down," and he huffed and he puffed and he blew the house down, and the little pig ran away.'

'He ate the little pig,' said William.

'No, no,' said Granny. 'The little pig ran away.'

'He ate the little pig. He ate her in a sandwich.'

'All right, he ate the little pig in a sandwich. So the second little pig – '

'You didn't tell about the tricycle.'

'What about the tricycle?'

'The wolf got on his tricycle and went to the bread shop to buy some bread. To make the sandwich,' William explained, patiently.

'Oh well, the wolf got on his tricycle and went to the bread shop to buy some bread. And he went to the grocer's to buy some butter.' This innovation did not go down well.

'He already had some butter in the cupboard,' said William.

'So then the second little pig went for a walk and met a man with a load of wood, and the little pig said to the man, "May I have some of that wood to build a house?" and the man said, "Yes."'

'He didn't say please.'

'"Please may I have some of that wood to build a house?"'

'It was sticks.'

'Sticks *are* wood.'

William took out his book and turned the pages. 'That's right,' he said.

'Why don't you tell the story?' said Granny.

'I can't remember it,' said William.

'You could read it out of your book.'

'I've lost it,' said William, clutching his pullover.

'Look, do you know who this is?' He pulled a green angora scarf from under the sofa.

'No, who is it?' said Granny, glad of the diversion.

'This is Doctor Snake.' He made the scarf wriggle across the carpet.

'Why is he a doctor?'

'Because he is all furry,' said William. He wrapped the doctor round his neck and sat sucking the loose end. 'Go on about the wolf.'

'So the little pig built a house of sticks and along came the wolf – on his tricycle?'

'He came by bus. He didn't have any money for a ticket so he ate up the conductor.'

'That wasn't very nice of him,' said Granny.

'No,' said William. 'It wasn't *very* nice.'

'And the wolf said, "Little pig, little pig, let me come in," and the little pig said, "No," and the wolf said, "Then I'll huff and I'll puff and I'll blow your house down," so he huffed and he puffed and he blew the house down. And then what did he do?' Granny asked, cautiously.

William was silent.

'Did he eat the second little pig?'

'Yes.'

'How did he eat this little pig?' said Granny, prepared for more pig sandwiches or possibly pig on toast.

'With his mouth,' said William.

'Now the third little pig went for a walk and met a man with a load of bricks. And the little pig said, "*Please* may I have some of those bricks to build a house?" and the man said, "Yes." So the little pig took the bricks and built a house.'

'He built it on the bomb-site.'

'Next door to the wolf?' said Granny. 'That was very silly of him.'

'There wasn't anywhere else,' said William. 'All the roads were full up.'

'The wolf didn't have to come by bus or tricycle this time, then, did he?' said Granny, grown cunning.

'Yes.' William took out the book and peered in, secretively. 'He was playing in the cemetery. He had to get another bus.'

'And did he eat the conductor this time?'

'No. A nice man gave him some money, so he bought a ticket.'

'I'm glad to hear it,' said Granny.

'He ate the nice man,' said William.

'So the wolf got off the bus and went up to the little pig's house, and he said, "Little pig, little pig, let me come in," and the little pig said, "No," and then the wolf said, "I'll huff and I'll puff and I'll blow your house down," and he huffed and he puffed and he huffed and he puffed but he couldn't blow the house down because it was made of bricks.'

'He couldn't blow it down,' said William, 'because it was stuck to the ground.'

'Well, anyway, the wolf got very cross then, and he climbed on the roof and shouted down the chimney, "I'm coming to get you!" but the little pig just laughed and put a big saucepan of water on the fire.'

'He put it on the gas stove.'

'He put it on the *fire*,' said Granny, speaking very rapidly, 'and the wolf fell down the chimney and into the pan of water and was boiled and the little pig ate him for supper.'

William threw himself full length on the carpet and screamed.

'He didn't! He didn't! *He didn't*! He didn't eat the wolf.'

Granny picked him up, all stiff and kicking, and sat him on her lap.

'Did I get it wrong again, love? Don't cry. Tell me what really happened.'

William wept, and wiped his nose on Doctor Snake.

'The little pig put the saucepan on the gas stove and the wolf got down the chimney and put the little pig in the saucepan and boiled him. He had him for tea, with chips,' said William.

'Oh,' said Granny. 'I've got it all wrong, haven't I? Can I see the book, then I shall know, next time.'

William took the book from under his pullover. Granny opened it and read, *First Aid for Beginners: a Practical Handbook*.

'I see,' said Granny. 'I don't think I can read this. I left my glasses at home. You tell Gran how it ends.'

William turned to the last page which showed a prostrate man with his leg in a splint; *compound fracture of the femur*.

'Then the wolf washed up and got on his tricycle and went to see his Granny, and his Granny opened the door and said, "Hello, William."'

'I thought it was the wolf.'

'It was. It was the wolf. His name was William Wolf,' said William.

'What a nice story,' said Granny. 'You tell it much better than I do.'

'I can see up your nose,' said William. 'It's all whiskery.'

You are not told William's character. You have to guess what is going on in his mind from what he says.

⇨ In small groups, discuss the following.

1 What can you deduce about William from these phrases?

C.A.T. wheelbarrow.
You make bacon out of dead pigs.
This is Doctor Snake.
I don't mind if it has cold feet.
He ate the nice man.
He didn't! He didn't!
I can see up your nose. It's all whiskery.

2 Is Granny spoiling William? Why might she be especially nice to him? What is worrying him most?
3 Who is William's hero in the story?
4 Which of these adjectives apply to William: funny, silly, sensitive, rude, cruel, clever, deceitful? Give examples from the story.

⇨ On your own, write about someone you know in such a way that the reader can discover his or her character without being told. It does not have to be a child. Describe what he or she does or says, or perhaps an incident where their character is shown.

Re-write a fairy tale

The story is called 'William's Version' because it is so changed from the original. The wolf is William's hero and he does things that William is familiar with – he plays in the cemetery, rides a bicycle and goes on buses, for instance.

 Write a version of another fairy tale that you think might interest William or children like him. Remember to include some features of modern life. For example, Red Riding Hood might visit her Granny in a helicopter and the pilot could be a wolf.

FOOTNOTE

If you use *for instance* or *for example* in a sentence, comma it off. Notice how it has been done on this page. This is one use of the comma.

SPELL WELL

bread bead read head headache lead plead

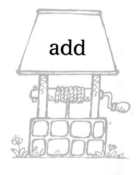

ladder addition sadder adder cladding

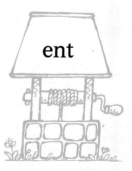

moment comment advent imminent spent transparent

GET YOURSELF HEARD

18

We continue our look at letters with some written by students of your own age. There is plenty to get you talking here. The letters were published in the children's newspaper *Early Times*.

Pollution problem

THREE weeks ago there was a huge downpour, and all of the water ran off the surrounding fields and flowed down a small stream into our pond.

Soon after we noticed that the pond was a red/brown colour and when I went out in our boat and stirred up the bottom with an oar, a pink cloud rose to the surface!

It seemed to me that chemicals used as fertilizers had been washed off the fields and settled at the bottom of our pond.

Since we noticed the colour change three days ago I have had to drag three dead carp from the pond.

Not only have we lost our fish but we have four ducks and a couple of moorhens who fed from the pond daily.

My sisters Nicola and Rebecca and a friend have been down to the pond recently and it is very upsetting to see a beautiful piece of nature ruined by man's carelessness. Is there anything we can do to stop the same happening elsewhere?

**Marcus Milliner, 14,
from Wadhurst, Sussex.**

Ideas about ID

I AM writing in reply to Chris Cooke's letter in Platform issue 58. I totally agree with the idea about identity cards for people.

I am 13-years-old and recently I went to Paris with my family and some sixth-formers from our school, most of them were under 18.

Entry to museums and national monuments was free to under 18s. We were caught out at the Palace of Versailles because many (for safe-keeping) had left their passports in the hotel – our only means of identification.

Even though I, for one, don't look very old, the staff in the museum made me pay along with the other under 18-year-olds.

If carrying identity cards were compulsory we wouldn't have been caught in this position.

After that incident we started to carry our passports with us everywhere in Paris.

Susie Barnes, 13,
from Cambs.

The Royals

I AM writing in reply to Andrew Watts' letter (ET No. 34)

In it he talked about the way the Royals earn their salaries.

Personally I do not see it is fair that one family can have the special treatment they do, just by accident of birth.

This however is just a part. I was very angry to see the way he talked about the unemployed as 'layabout yobbos'.

This is an insult to the majority who would certainly work if the opportunity arose.

Most football hooligans have well paid jobs and fight on the terraces as a game to play at weekends.

I hope the correspondent will think about his comments that put down three million of the British population.

Rosamond Allen, 13,
from St Ives, Cambridge.

Bullying relief

I AM writing to say how glad my family are that someone has noticed bullying at school (ET 78).

It is a horrible matter and I feel deeply concerned as my younger brother who is seven is bullied but not in the drastic way mentioned in the article.

The thing that concerns me is that usually the children being bullied are forced to move schools. I don't think this is fair.

Fiona McGregor, 11,
from Sandy, Bedfordshire.

▭ In small groups, discuss the issues raised in the letters. How far do you agree with the writers? Have you any examples from personal experience which would help you to argue for or against their views?

▭ Write either a reply to one of the letters or a letter raising an issue of your own.

▭ Look at Karen's letter – the last one. Compare it to the others. This was not accepted for publication. Why do you think it was rejected? Discuss in your groups the reasons an editor might give for not publishing Karen's letter.

Why crimes should be punished more severely

Criminals commit crime knowing that they will only get a fine or imprisonment for a few months or a year.

Some criminals get away without a proper punishment even though they are guilty.

When criminals have finished their punishment they start to commit crime again. This happens usually after they have paid a fine. To most people it doesn't matter about money.To them it is a way to commit crime and pay, like buying a licence to commit crime the only difference is that you get the licence after committing a crime.

Criminals are usually linked up to a gang or a professional group. People commit crime because they are not punished severely enough. I think torture should be brought in. This sounds blood-thirsty but I have good reasons.

Torture is rather efficient because criminals who are being punished have a scar of terrible pain on their characters for all their lives.

If criminals pay a fine they can clear their name, but when they have been tortured they can feel the pain that they brought upon others.

Torture would be very good on murderers because if they have been imprisoned or fined it does not make any difference to them. Paying a fine is simple. Being put in prison is even simpler because they get fed. They have a roof over their heads and they even get free advice from criminals who are a few steps higher up the ladder. Torture gives them pain only pain. Nobody else gets hurt. This is very good for murderers, child abusers, rapists and muggers. These villains all cause pain to people who are more dependent than themselves. This is why they deserve pain; the pain they use on others. If criminals are hanged they might be someone innocent. If an innocent person was tortured at least they would not be dead. They could be paid a compensation later when they had evidence of their innocence.

When a person is murdered the murderer does not know the grief and pain the family has to go through. Torture is a taste of their own medicine.

Karen

103

HOW TO USE A THESAURUS

19

This Step is about a very important tool to help you with your English. It is a book called a **thesaurus**. Now read on . . .

Pick the best word

One advantage writing has over speaking is that we can have time to pick the right word to get the exact meaning we want. We can also vary the words we use and not repeat ourselves. The same word used again and again can become boring. The most useful book you can use to help you find the right words is a thesaurus. The most popular is called *Roget's Thesaurus*.

Suppose, as a task, your teacher asked you to write about *a cold winter's day*. First look at the index at the *back* of the thesaurus. If you were looking for *cold* and *winter* you would find them on the thesaurus pages shown opposite.

You can now look up both *winter* under section 129 and *coldness* under section 380. Note they are sections and not pages. The sections are at the front of the book. The two sections are shown on page 106.

You will know some of the words. That is one job of the thesaurus, to remind you of words you already know. Some of the words will be new to you, but from now on you can start using some of them. Once you have found a new word it is amazing how quickly you see or hear it used in a book or on the TV. Your teacher will soon tell you if you are not using the new word quite correctly.

col
narrowness 206 n.
high land 209 n.
cold
wintry 129 adj.
dead 361 adj.
unfeeling 375 adj.
coldness 380 n.
cold 380 adj.
cooled 382 adj.
blue 435 adj.
mistaken 495 adj.
infection 651 n.
respiratory disease
651 n.
uncooked 670 adj.
refreshing 685 adj.
adversity 731 n.
impassive 820 adj.
inexcitable 823 adj.
cheerless 834 adj.
indifferent 860 adj.
inimical 881 adj.
unsociable 883 adj.
unkind 898 adj.
pure 950 adj.
cold-blooded
animal 365 adj.
impassive 820 adj.
cautious 858 adj.
unastonished
865 adj.
cruel 898 adj.
cold comfort
discontent 829 n.
cold cream
cleanser 648 n.
cosmetic 843 n.
cold-eyed
cruel 898 adj.
cold feet
nervousness 854 n.
cold fish
unfeeling person
820 n.
cold frame
garden 370 n.
cold front
wintriness 380 n.
cold-hearted
impassive 820 adj.
selfish 932 adj.
cold light of day
disclosure 526 n.
coldness
coldness 380 n.
(See cold)
cold-shoulder
exclude 57 vb.
repel 292 vb.
disregard 458 vb.
rejection 607 n.
reject 607 vb.
avoid 620 vb.
make unwelcome
883 vb.
be rude 885 vb.
cold-shouldered
friendless 883 adj.

cold shower
moderator 177 n.
ablutions 648 n.
cold steel
lunge 712 n.
sidearms 723 n.
cold storage
delay 136 n.
refrigeration 382 n.
refrigerator 384 n.
preservation 666 n.
cold sweat
fear 854 n.
cold turkey
drug-taking 949 n.
cold war
peace 717 n.
war 718 n.
cold water
moderator 177 n.
dissuasion 613 n.
cold wind
wind 352 n.
adversity 731 n.
coleslaw
hors-d'oeuvres 301 n.
colic
pang 377 n.
digestive disorders
651
colitis
digestive disorders
65
collaborate
assent 488 vb.
be willing 597
apostatize 603
cooperate 706
collaboration
cooperation 7
collaborator
tergiversator
aider 703 n.
collaborato
toady 879
friend 880
collage
combinat
picture 5
collapse
decomp
cease 1
helples
be im
weak
ruin
desc
desc
illn
be
di
d
f

collar
halter 47 n.
garment 228 n.
neckwear 228 n.
arrest 747 vb.
fetter 748 n.
take 786 vb.
collar stud
jewellery 844 n.
collate
co...... 462 vb.
pr
col
k

collective noun
assemblage 74 n.
part of speech 564 n.
collectivism
government 733 n.
joint possession
775 n.
collector
accumulator 74 n.
collector 492 n.
enthusiast 504 n.
desirer 859 n.
...ctor's piece

wing commander
air officer 741 n.
winged
flying 271 adj.
speedy 277 adj.
wings
livery 547 n.
stage set 594 n.
theatre 594 n.
wingspan
breadth 205 n.
wink
look 438 n.
be blind 439 vb.
be dim-sighted
440 vb.
hint 524 n.vb.
indication 547 n.
gesticulate 547 vb.
warning 664 n.
excite love 887 vb.
approve 923 vb.
— at
disregard 458 vb.
permit 756 vb.
winker
signal light 420 n.
indicator 547 n.
winkle
fish food 301 n.
marine life 365 n.
winkle out
extract 304 vb.
winner
superior 34 n.
exceller 644 n.
victor 727 n.
recipient 782 n.
winning
superior 34 adj.
successful 727 adj.
pleasurable 826 adj.
amiable 884 adj.
lovable 887 adj.
winning post
limit 236 n.
objective 617 n.
winnings
gain 771 n.
receipt 807 n.
winning ways
inducement 612 n.
lovableness 887 n.
winnow
eliminate 44 vb.
aerate 340 vb.
cultivate 370 vb.
enquire 459 vb.
select 605 vb.
wino
drunkard 949 n.
winsome
personable 841 adj.
lovable 887 adj.
winter
pass time 108 vb.
period 110 n.
winter 129 n.
wintriness 380 n.

adversity 731 n.
winter sports
snow 380 n.
sport 837 n.
wintry
wintry 129 adj.
cold 380 adj.
wipe
dry 342 vb.
touch 378 vb.
clean 648 vb.
— away one's tears
relieve 831 vb.
pity 905 vb.
— out
nullify 2 vb.
destroy 165 vb.
slaughter 362 vb.
obliterate 550 vb.
— the floor with
defeat 727 vb.
— the slate clean
forgive 909 vb.
wire
cable 47 n.
narrowness 206 n.
filament 208 n.
information 524 n.
message 529 n.
telecommunication
531 n.
wiredraw
lengthen 203 vb.
make thin 206 vb.
wireless
broadcasting 531 n.
(See radio)
wire netting
network 222 n.
wire-puller
latency 523 n.
motivator 612 n.
director 690 n.
slyboots 698 n.
wire-pulling
influence 178 n.
plot 623 n.
wire-tapping
listening 415 n.
wireworm
creepy-crawly 365 n.
wiry
stalwart 162 adj.
lean 206 adj.
fibrous 208 adj.
wisdom
thought 449 n.
erudition 490 n.
wisdom 498 n.
caution 858 n.
wise
judicial 480 adj.
knowing 490 adj.
aphoristic 496 adj.
wise 498 adj.
foreseeing 510 adj.
way 624 n.
advisable 642 adj.
skilful 694 adj.

cunning 698 adj.
cautious 858 adj.
wise after the event
ill-timed 138 adj.
wisecrack
witticism 839 n.
be witty 839 vb.
wised-up
informed 524 adj.
wise guy
sciolist 493 n.
wiseacre 500 n.
affecter 850 n.
wise man
sage 500 n.
sorcerer 983 n.
wiser
improved 654 adj.
wise to
knowing 490 adj.
wise woman
sage 500 n.
sorceress 983 n.
wish
will 595 n.
request 761 n.
desire 859 n., vb.
desired object 859 n.
— on
desire 859 vb.
curse 899 vb.
— one joy
congratulate 886 vb.
— to sink through
the floor
be humbled 872 vb.
— undone
regret 830 vb.
dislike 861 vb.
be penitent 939 vb.
— well
be benevolent
897 vb.
wishbone
magic instrument
983 n.
wish fulfilment
content 828 n.
wishful thinking
misjudgment 481 n.
credulity 487 n.
error 495 n.
fantasy 513 n.
deception 542 n.
hope 852 n.
wishing well
magic instrument
983 n.
wishy-washy
weak 163 adj.
tasteless 387 adj.
feeble 572 adj.
wisp
insubstantial thing
4 n.
small thing 33 n.
piece 53 n.
bunch 74 n.
thinness 206 n.

filament 208 n.
hair 259 n.
wispy
fragmentary 53 adj.
flimsy 163 adj.
wisteria
tree 366 n.
wistful
regretting 830 adj.
desiring 859 adj.
wit
intelligence 498 n.
humorist 839 n.
wit 839 n.
ridiculousness 849 n.
witch
old woman 133 n.
a beauty 841 n.
eyesore 842 n.
hellhag 904 n.
fairy 970 n.
sorceress 983 n.
witchcraft
diabolism 969 n.
sorcery 983 n.
witch doctor
sage 500 n.
doctor 658 n.
sorcerer 983 n.
priest 986 n.
witchery
inducement 612 n.
pleasurableness
826 n.
sorcery 983 n.
witch-hunt
enquiry 459 n.
search 459 n.
pursuit 619 n.
defame 926 vb.
witch-hunting
phobia 854 n.
orthodox 976 adj.
witching
magical 983 adj.
sorcerous 983 adj.
witenagemot
parliament 692 n.
with
in addition 38 adv.
among 43 adv.
conjointly 45 adv.
with 89 adv.
by means of
629 adv.
with a bad grace
unwillingly 598 adv.
sullenly 893 adv.
wih a good grace
willingly 597 adv.
with an eye to
purposely 617 adv.
with a pinch of salt
provided 468 adv.
doubtfully 486 adv.
with a vengeance
extremely 32 adv.
crescendo 36 adv.
in addition 38 adv.

man, Romanesque, Gothic, Tudor, Elizabethan, Jacobean, Georgian, Regency, Victorian; historical 125 *past*, 866 *renowned*.

primal, prime, primitive, primeval, primordial, aboriginal 68 *beginning*; geological, preglacial, fossil, palaeozoic 110 *secular*; eolithic, palaeolithic, mesolithic, neolithic; early, proto-, dawn-, eo-; antemundane, pre-adamite, antediluvian.

immemorial, ancestral, traditional, time-

fingered Dawn; daystar, orb of day 321 *sun*.

noon, high noon, meridian, midday, noonday, noontide; eight bells, twelve o'clock.

spring, springtime, springtide, Eastertide, vernal season, spring s., seed-time, blossom-time, maying; first cuckoo; vernal equinox, first point of Aries.

summer 379 *heat*; summertime, summertide, Whitsuntide; midsummer, summer solstice, Midsummer's Day, high summer, dog days; haymaking; aestivation; Indian summer, St Luke's s., St Martin's s.

Adj. *matinal*, matutinal, morning; diurnal, daytime; auroral, dawning, fresh, dewy 135 *early*; antemeridian; noon, meridian.

vernal, equinoctial, spring; springlike, sappy, juicy, flowering, florescent 130 *young*.

summery, summer, aestival 379 *warm*.

Adv. *at sunrise*, at dawn of day, at first light, at crack of dawn; with the lark; past midnight, in the small hours; a.m.

See: 66, 130, 135, 321, **379**, **417**.

129 Evening. Autumn. Winter

N. *evening*, eventide, even, eve, dewy e.; evensong, vespers, afternoon, p.m.; matinée; afternoon tea, five o'clock; sundowner, soirée; dog-watches; sunset, sundown, setting sun, going down of the sun; evening star, Hesperus, Vesper; dusk, crepuscule, twilight, gloaming 419 *half-light*; candlelight, cockshut, dewfall; moonrise, moonset 321 *moon*; close of day, nightfall, dark, blind man's holiday, nighttime, night-owl 418 *darkness*; bedtime 679 *sleep*; curfew, last post 136 *lateness*, 69 *finality*.

midnight, dead of night, witching time; night-watch, small hours.

autumn, back-end, fall, fall of the leaf; harvest, harvest-time; harvest moon, hunter's m.; Michaelmas; Indian summer; autumnal equinox; 'season of mists and mellow fruitfulness'.

winter 380 *wintriness*; wintertime, wintertide; yuletide, Christmas; midwinter, winter solstice; hibernation.

Adj. *vespertine*, afternoon, postmeridian; vesperal, evening; dusky, crepuscular 418 *dark*, 419 *dim*; nightly, nocturnal, noctivagant; benighted, late; bedtime.

fire, take f., draw; blaze, flare, flame, flame up, burst into flame, go up in flames; glow, flush; smoke, smoulder, reek, fume, steam 300 *emit*; boil, seethe 318 *effervesce*; toast, grill, roast, sizzle, crackle, frizzle, fry, bake 381 *burn*; get burnt, scorch, boil dry; bask, sun oneself, sunbathe; get sunburnt, tan; swelter, sweat, perspire, glow; melt, thaw 337 *liquefy*; stifle, parch 342 *be dry*; thirst, pant, gasp for breath, fight for air; be in a fever, be feverish, have a fever, run a temperature; keep warm, wrap up.

See: 128, 300, 318, 337, 342, 364, 376, **381**, 383, 388, **417**, **420**, 431, 651, 653, 723, 981.

380 Cold

N. *coldness*, low temperature, drop in t.; cool, coolness, freshness; cold, freezing c., zero temperature, zero, absolute z.; freezing point; frigidity, gelidity; iciness, frostiness; sensation of cold, chilliness, algidity, rigour, hypothermia, shivering, shivers, chattering of the teeth, gooseflesh, goose pimples, frostbite, chilblains; chill, catching cold; cold climate, high latitudes, Frigid Zone, Siberia, North Pole, South P.; Arctic, Antarctica; snowline, permafrost; glacial epoch, Ice Age; polar bear, Eskimo.

wintriness, winter, depth of w., hard w., severe w.; nip in the air, cold snap; cold weather, cold front; inclemency, wintry weather, arctic conditions, polar temperature, degrees of frost; snowstorm, hailstorm, blizzard; frost, Jack Frost, frostwork, rime, hoarfrost, white frost, sharp f., hard f.; sleet, hail, hailstone, silver thaw, black ice, freeze.

snow, snowfall, snowflake, snow crystal; avalanche, snow slip, snowdrift; snowstorm, flurry of snow, the old woman plucking her geese; snowball, snowman; snowplough, snowshoe; winter sports 837 *sport*.

ice, dry i., ice cube; hailstone, icicle; ice cap, ice field, ice sheet, ice shelf, floe, ice f., iceberg, berg, ice front, glacier, icefall; serac; shelf ice, pack i.; driven snow, frozen s., névé, frozen sea; icebreaker, ice yacht; ice house, icebox 384 *refrigerator*; ice action, glaciation 382 *refrigeration*; glaciology.

Adj. *cold*, without heat, impervious to heat, adiathermanous; cool, temperate; shady,

chill, chilly, parky, nippy; unheated, unwarmed, unthawed; fresh, raw, keen, bitter, nipping, biting, piercing; inclement, freezing, gelid, ice-cold, bitterly c., below zero; frigid, brumal 129 *wintry*; winterbound, frosty, frostbound, snowy, snow-covered, mantled in snow, blanketed in s.; slushy, sleety, icy; glacial, ice-capped, glaciered, glaciated; boreal, polar, arctic, Siberian.

chilly, feeling cold, acold; shivering, chattering, shivery, algid, aguish; blue, blue with cold; shrammed, perished, perishing, starved with cold, chilled to the bone, frozen, frostbitten, frost-nipped; like ice, cold as charity, cold as a frog, cold as marble, stone-cold, cold as death.

Vb. *be cold*, - chilly etc. adj.; grow cold, lose heat, drop in temperature; feel cold, chatter, shiver, tremble, shake, quake, quiver, shudder; freeze, starve, perish with cold; catch cold, get a chill; chill 382 *refrigerate*.

Adv. *frostily*, frigidly, bitterly, coldly.

See: 129, **382**, 384, 837.

381 Heating

N. *heating*, superheating, increase of temperature, calefaction, torrefaction; diathermy; diathermancy; transcalency; calorific value, thermal efficiency; warming, keeping warm; space heating, central h., district heating system 383 *heater*; insolation, sunning 342 *desiccation*; melting, thawing 337 *liquefaction*; smelting, scorification, cupellation; boiling, ebullition; baking, cooking 301 *cookery*; decoction, distillation; antifreeze mixture.

burning, combustion; inflammation, kindling, ignition; reheat, afterburning; deflagration, conflagration 379 *fire*; incineration, calcination; roasting; cremation 364 *interment*; suttee, self-burning 362 *suicide*; auto-da-fé, holocaust 981 *oblation*; cauterization, cautery, branding; scorching, singeing, charring, carbonization; inflammability, combustibility; burner 383 *furnace*; cauterizer, caustic, moxa, vitriol; hot iron, branding i., brand; match, touchpaper 385 *lighter*; stoker, fireman; burn mark, burn, brand, singe, scald, sunburn, tan.

incendiarism, arson, fire-raising, pyromania; incendiary, arsonist, fire-raiser, fire-bug; firebrand, revolutionary 738 *agitator*.

➦ In the following piece you are given a choice of three words. Pick the one you think fits in the best and write out the whole piece:

	bleak		pedalled		tortuous
The day was	dreary	as Janine	cycled	down the long	twisting
	raw		biked		winding

	pond		smiled	
lane to the	lake	. The sun had not	shone	for three days
	water		appeared	

	clamminess		air	
and there was a	dampness	in the	atmosphere. This gave a
	moistness		weather	

	strangeness		flora and fauna	
certain	eeriness	to the	countryside	It was a day
	bleakness		landscape	

	think about	
in which you could	imagine	strange creatures in your
	conjure up	

thoughts
mind   . There had been newspaper reports of something
imagination

	roaming		forests	
	lurking	in the	woods	around Selsdon Chase and ten sheep
	wandering		spinneys	

107

<pre>
                      torn out
had had their throats ripped out at Manor Farm.
                      gored

              inky   rushed out   copse
Suddenly a(n) black   shape shot out   of the hedgerow on
              sombre   sprang out   bushes

the left. It was at least five feet long and seemed liked

    massive
a giant   dog.
    huge

        careered   smashed
Janine swerved left and crashed   into a blackberry bush.
        swung   slammed

                 spectre   rushed
Thoughts of Shuki the ghost   dog swam   through her
                 apparition   percolated

        gazing   heavenwards
mind as she lay looking upwards
        peering   skywards
</pre>

⟶ Look in your thesaurus to find other words for:

Verbs: cry, laugh, run, kill, get (acquire)
Adjectives: big, little, great (goodness), nasty (not nice).

Get the thesaurus habit when writing.

SPELL WELL

sign signature ignore benign

harmful army farmer armistice

hive lively striven contrive

JUST AS IT HAPPENED

You have done well to get this far. We finish with a West Indian story. We ask you only one question, but you may like to discuss the story with your friends.

The best stories are often from direct personal experience – a detailed record of a happy or sad event from your own life.

Read this sad story of Banjo's very short life, written by Denis Foster. Notice how much detail we are given of the catching and killing of Banjo. This detail has obviously been impressed on the writer's mind. It all helps the reader to share the writer's feelings.

Banjo

Banjo lived and died in obscurity. Born on the street, he died on the street. Found in a garbage bin, his remains now rot in a garbage disposal dump.

He lived for three months, and in that time he made Helen and myself and a few others very happy, and caused no one any pain.

When I found Banjo, he was a weak and wiry little puppy, suspicious of all people, and very afraid of them. His ribs hung down in streaks from his back like banjo strings, and his head, which was all eyes, was ten times too big for his body. It rested precariously on his shoulders, and his ears perched on his head like floppy birds on a branch.

The first time I approached this little brown dog, he scrambled out of the overturned garbage bin, and stumbled, with his tail tucked between his bony legs, and his head turned warily in my direction, under the car whining. Every time I approached him, he would shift his position cleverly – moving from under one wheel to the other. I knew that he was afraid of me, but he also knew that I was afraid of him. He knew that I did not want to frighten or startle him in my effort to catch him. He knew, I think, that I did not want to chase him away. What he did not understand, was why.

And so, he circled me, and I circled him from bumper to bumper. Eventually, after enticing him with a bowl of milk and stale bread, which he wisely refused, I gave up the chase and went upstairs to the kitchen resigned to the fact that I had been outwitted. Through the window I saw his spindly legs carry him bouncing down the drive and out into the street. Impulsively I ran downstairs after him. He had strolled into the next-door neighbour's yard and was nonchalantly smelling around behind the low entrance wall. I crept closer. He was rustling in the grass behind the wall, occupied, not expecting me to strike back, especially in somebody else's yard. I stepped softly, slowly, crouching slightly behind the wall, with only my head showing. Now we were opposite each other; he on one side of the wall, I on the other. There he was backing me, completely unaware of my presence. Then in a flash, my hands were down upon him. He jumped and tried to wriggle out of my grasp, yelping, his head waving madly, in utter disbelief and confusion.

In the living room of our house there was a large couch which was pushed up against a wall. And it was here that Banjo spent his first week with us. He was very much afraid of his new surroundings, and still very suspicious of our motives. He would sit behind the couch all day without revealing himself, and every time we approached him he would shiver all over like a vibrating banjo string.

At first Banjo would eat nothing. We tried bread soaked in milk, and when he refused that, we tried milk and eggs; but he would have none of it. He was so young and starved that we thought we should wean him gradually on to harder food. However, after the first day of trying in vain to get him to eat, we became desperate, thinking that he would die at any moment. That night after dinner, however, our worries came to an end. We had eaten oxtail stew for dinner, and I put the left-over bones in a plate next to the couch, just as a last resort, not thinking him old enough to eat such food. To my surprise, when Banjo thought we were not looking he sneaked out from under the couch, and one by one the bones disappeared into his cave of solitude.

The next morning when I offered him some more bones, I held one in my hand, and pushed it in front of Banjo's nose. He cocked his huge head to one side and eyed me inquiringly. He did not quite understand this macabre game. I wanted him out from behind the couch, he was aware of that much; but he was still too wary of human beings to realize that what I really wanted was to build up some sort of friendly relationship with him.

Hunger, however, makes a fool of man and dog alike, and eventually he took his first bone, shaking all over, from my hand.

From that moment our relationship developed. By the end of the first week he had ceased to live like a hermit and was walking, however unsteadily, around the house investigating every corner like a determined Sherlock Holmes.

The day soon came when Banjo followed us everywhere we went in the house.

Then the day of decision came. We opened the doors to Banjo for the first time since we had found him. He was free to stay or go. We watched him intently through the kitchen window as he sniffed his way slowly down the drive. He reached the gate, and there he sat down and contemplated the public road. He turned around, sat down again, and contemplated his surroundings. He looked back at the road outside, wagged his tail, and came pelting up the drive and into the house.

The last time I saw Banjo alive was around 7 o'clock one Sunday evening. We were watching television, and it was not until about one hour later that I really began to worry about him. I thought maybe he was next door.

I walked out into the front yard and whistled and called for him from the gate. But I did not hear the characteristic patter of his tiny feet. I walked out in the street. In the middle of the road lay a dark mass, a shadow.

I knew it was Banjo. I knew too that he was dead. I had never really expected to find him dead. Death was always something separate from life, something distant and fantastic. I bent down beside the body. His hind legs were spraddled out behind him and his body was bloated. There was a large gash along his stomach, not a puncture, but the skin had been ripped off and I saw the black tyre squeezing and pinching the flesh against the tar road. I saw the wheel turning over and the body being sucked under. The flattening lungs suddenly gasped. I felt the backbone and the ribs under the tyre, and the black rubber giving slightly as the bones snapped and splayed open and the guts squelched and burst inside the stretching skin. I heard the stifled cry that was drowned out by the drone of the motor. . . .

The body lay on the road cold and distorted.

A man on a bicycle rode slowly down the road singing a happy indifferent tune to himself and the shadows of the night. I remembered standing on Mt Hillaby that morning listening to the church bells ringing in some distant valley.

I removed the collar from around Banjo's neck and hopelessly began to cry.

▭▷Do you think that writing about it gets you through a period of sadness?

Language words

A list of words and terms to do with language follows. Go through them and consult with your teacher about any you are not sure of or have forgotten. The number after the words refers to where they are first mentioned in this book.

genres (page 12)
plot (19)
dialogue (19)
playscript (19)
stage directions (19)
acts (19)
scenes (19)
dramatic (20)
character (20)
abbreviate/abbreviation (21)
apostrophe (21)
audience (21)
layout (22)
punctuate/punctuation (22)
drafting (22)
re-drafting (22)
dialect (25)
accent (25)
Standard English (25)
alphabetical order (35)
noun (39)

poem/poetry (42)
prose (44)
rhyme (45)
rhythm (45)
syllable (45)
limerick (46)
narrative (47)
speech marks (inverted commas) (52)
paragraph (58)
indent (59)
proper noun (61)
bias (66)
note-taking (69)
present tense (70)
past tense (70)
adjectives (73)
transcription (76)
pronoun (78)
block capitals (80)
topic sentence (82)
thesaurus (104)